HOW TO MAKE *anything* IN AN AIR FRYER

HOW TO MAKE *anything* IN AN AIR FRYER

100 quick, easy and delicious recipes

HAYLEY DEAN

EBURY
PRESS

CONTENTS

INTRODUCTION

WELCOME TO HAYLEY'S WORLD

HELLO,
I'M HAYLEY...

It's really nice to meet you here. Thank you so much for picking up my first cookbook. Some of you might already know me from my posts on Instagram and TikTok, but for those of you who don't then let me introduce myself.

I'm a busy (single) mum of two daughters who loves cooking and sharing my recipes online. What started as a hobby over eight years ago has now turned into my full-time career and I couldn't be more pleased (and surprised) about that!

I love being able to channel my creativity into the kitchen and the meals that I create. And now I get to share my recipes with you in this book. I'm a home cook who is entirely self-taught, I haven't trained as a professional chef but my natural passion for food has allowed me to learn SO much along the way.

Because I don't have endless amounts of time to spend shopping and cooking, and I need to get the kids fed each day, everything I cook is really achievable. I create simple recipes that anyone can follow and get great results, even in the smallest kitchen.

As you will have gathered from the title of this book, it's an air-fryer cookbook. Air fryers are taking over the food world at the moment, but I don't believe they're some kind of fad – they're here to stay.

Air fryers are being used in the place of conventional ovens to make more and more meals every day. I absolutely love my air fryer. I use it to cook everything, from sausages, burgers and bacon to garlic bread, toasties, chips and even cookies... plus so much more!

I really hope you enjoy cooking the recipes in this book. Please do share them with me on social media as I would love to see what you create. Thank you and see you soon!

WHY I LOVE MY AIR FRYER

One of the best things about an air fryer is that they cook food faster and more efficiently than a normal oven. They can also be much cheaper to run as they use less energy and only need to be on for a shorter period of time. Air fryers work by blasting hot air all around the food you place inside it. Depending on the make and model of your air fryer, it may have multiple settings, including a bake, roast and grill function. In this book, however, I use the standard air-fryer mode for every recipe to keep things simple.

What model to buy...

There are lots of different brands of air fryers around: there are some at the cheaper end that are limited to the basic functions and then there are some more pricey ones that offer more settings and other gadgets to go with them. There are also some machines with two drawers, which can be useful if you're cooking different types of food at the same time. Personally, I prefer to use an air fryer with one large drawer as they tend to have a larger internal space and work great for cakes, crumbles, sharing desserts in general, as well as traybakes, pizzas and roasts!

Whichever machine you choose, it's totally up to your own personal preference – just think about how you'll use your air fryer and what kind of dishes you'll make the most. You might decide that you want to spend a bit more on an air fryer with multiple functions, but don't feel that you have to. At least, you don't have to in order to make any of my recipes in this book. When it comes to price, I find the cheaper machines cook just as well as the higher-priced models and so I've devised all my recipes so they can be cooked in regular air-fryer mode.

When to line the air fryer

When you're cooking food in an air fryer, you don't really need to line the basket or drawer – everything will cook perfectly well in an unlined air fryer. Whenever I mention lining the air fryer in a recipe, it's usually to prevent the air fryer from getting too dirty or to stop small pieces of food from falling down the holes in the plate that allow the hot air to circulate. Using a liner is not strictly necessary, but I do feel that a liner protects the air fryer and makes cleaning up a lot easier – so it's a win-win.

When preheating your air fryer, never line the drawer or basket with a paper air-fryer liner without first placing something on top of the liner to weight it down. Paper liners can float upwards in the hot air and touch the heating element, meaning that it could potentially catch fire. ALWAYS add the paper liner to the air fryer after preheating. Rather than using a paper liner, I strongly recommend using a silicone liner, kitchen foil or oven-safe, heatproof trays and dishes.

Check the temperature

All air fryers vary slightly on temperature and cooking time, so make sure you use my timings and temperatures as a guide and always check the food while it's cooking by simply opening the air fryer drawer or basket and taking a look. If you're new to air-frying, you'll quickly get used to your machine by a little trial and error; they're so easy to use though that you'll be fine in no time!

The use of a digital probe thermometer is also a good idea so that you can check the internal temperature of dishes to make sure they're fully cooked. If you don't own one already, a probe thermometer is a great investment.

What you can and can't cook in an air fryer

There are some limitations to what an air fryer can do. For example, you can't cook pasta or rice (at least, not very well). Air fryers are best used to cook less 'wet' foods, especially those that naturally crisp up and turn golden, but there are many other things an air fryer cooks really well including vegetables, meat, bakes, desserts and so much more...

Another benefit is that when you are cooking those crispy, golden foods that you might ordinarily deep-fry, by cooking them in the air fryer you only need to use a very small amount of oil. Air-frying versus deep-frying is a much healthier option. I prefer to use a spray oil, either a vegetable oil or an olive oil, rather than the low-calorie spray oils that are available. As well as potentially containing various chemicals, these low-calorie spray oils can damage the non-stick coating of your air fryer. My top tip is to keep refilling a cheap spray bottle with your own vegetable or olive oil, rather than buy spray oil from the supermarket each time as they tend to be more expensive than a regular, non-spray bottle of oil.

Why I count calories

Although this isn't a diet book, I always give the approximate calorie counts for all my recipes as I know lots of my followers are interested in tracking what they eat. Most of the recipes in this book are less than 600 calories per serving. And because they're cooked in an air fryer, which requires less oil, that helps to keep the calorie count down – a good thing for those of us who are calorie conscious! While I don't follow any particular diet, by any means, I do like to keep an eye on what I'm eating each week and being aware of the calories I'm eating helps me do that. However, I don't get too hung up on it – my love of food is too strong!

MY ESSENTIAL INGREDIENTS

There are a number of storecupboard ingredients that I find invaluable and always keep in stock as they help me to whip up delicious meals with the minimum of fuss.

Mayonnaise

For me, mayonnaise is the king of condiments. There is always a bottle of squeezy mayo in my cupboard. I love it with chips, in burgers, in wraps, in sandwich fillings, as a salad dressing, and much more. It's incredibly versatile as you can mix it with other ingredients to vary the taste – I often flavour mayo with sriracha, pesto, chipotle paste, as well as using mayo as the base for tartare sauce, katsu sauce, ranch dressing and garlic dip. Instead of regular mayo, I prefer to use the 'light' version to cut back on a few calories.

Barbecue sauce

Barbecue sauce is not just a brilliant sauce for dipping chicken tenders into, it's also a really handy cheat ingredient. The spices and sugar in barbecue sauce make it an excellent glaze for meat. I use it when cooking gammon.

Hot sauce

There are a couple of hot sauces I always keep in the cupboard. Tabasco is great hot pepper sauce to splash into chillies or stews or onto chicken wings to add some heat. Originally from Thailand, sriracha chilli sauce is now found in every major supermarket. I love it with Asian-style dishes, such as fried rice.

Chilli jam

Even though it's called a jam, don't be fooled into thinking it's a sweet, fruity spread. Chilli jam is actually more of a savoury, spicy jelly that pairs brilliantly with meats and cheeses. I use it in burgers, burritos, bacon sandwiches and breakfast stacks. It's also brilliant with cheese.

Caramelised onion chutney

Sometimes called onion marmalade or onion jam, this chutney is packed with sticky, sweet, caramelised onions. It's a beautiful accompaniment to meats and cheeses. I spread it over flatbreads to make a quick, tasty snack and it's essential when making sausage rolls.

Garlic paste

While it's easy enough to make your own garlic paste by blitzing peeled garlic cloves with a little oil in a food processor, it's even easier to spoon exactly how much you need from a jar of ready-made paste. Plus it keeps for weeks.

Chopped tomatoes

Cans of chopped tomatoes are an ingredient that I always keep a stock of. They're just so useful, affordable and keep forever. If you buy the ones with mixed herbs already added then it saves you that step when cooking, just pour them straight into the pan.

Cheese slices

A melting cheese slice is essential on any burger. As there's just no way that I could ever cut cheese into slices as neatly as the ones you can buy, I save the time and effort by using pre-cut cheese slices.

Microwaveable rice

Pouches of microwaveable rice are a lifesaver for any cook who is short on time as they're ready to serve in just a few minutes. Usually the pouches contain enough for two servings, so I find there is absolutely nothing wasted.

Oven chips

I keep a bag of oven chips in the freezer for those days when I just don't have the time to peel spuds. What's even better is that they can be cooked from frozen, so I don't have to plan ahead.

Puff pastry

Another essential freezer ingredient, sheets of ready-rolled puff pastry are so convenient and versatile that I don't think I could do without them. Plus it cooks in minutes in the air fryer. Whether I'm making a savoury tart or a sweet pastry, I prefer the all-butter version for the flakiest, tastiest pastry.

CHAPTER 1

BREAKFAST & BRUNCH

DOUBLE SAUSAGE, EGG AND CHEESE BREAKFAST MUFFINS

SERVES 2

There's really no need to drag yourself to the drive thru this Sunday morning, you can make your favourite breakfast muffins even better at home. They're delicious served with a cold juice and a strong coffee for the perfect pick-me-up. The ultimate weekend treat!

Cooking time: 10 minutes

Preparation time: 5 minutes

Calories: 438 kcals per serving

For the muffins

4 reduced fat pork sausages

Non-stick spray oil

2 eggs

2 English muffins, sliced open

2 cheese slices

To serve

Your choice of ketchup or sauce

Preheat the air fryer to 180°C.

Remove the skins from the sausages, then form the sausagemeat from each one into a round patty.

Line the air fryer or spray with non-stick spray oil. Place the sausagemeat patties in the air fryer and cook for 5 minutes at 180°C.

Meanwhile, grease two small ramekins with spray oil and crack an egg into each one.

When the patties have been cooking for 5 minutes, flip the patties over, add the ramekins to the air fryer and cook both at 180°C for 4 minutes or until the eggs have set.

Once the sausage patties and eggs are cooked, remove them from the air fryer.

Put the sliced muffins in the air fryer for 1 minute to toast.

Finally, assemble the breakfast muffins with the sausage patties, cheese slices, fried eggs and your favourite sauce. I like to spread the base of the muffin with some tomato ketchup, then layer on two sausage patties with a cheese slice in between them, then topped off with the fried egg and the rest of the muffin.

EGGS BENEDICT

This recipe feels fancy, but it's actually super easy. Once you've mastered poaching eggs in the air fryer, there's no going back. The hollandaise sauce is equally easy to make – surprisingly so – and is absolutely delicious!

Cooking time: 15 minutes

Preparation time: 10 minutes

Calories: 534 kcals per serving

For the eggs

Non-stick spray oil

4 eggs

2 bacon medallions (or ham slices)

2 English muffins, sliced

For the hollandaise sauce

2 egg yolks

1 tablespoon fresh lemon juice

Small pinch cayenne pepper

60g 'light' salted butter

COOK'S TIP

All air fryers vary slightly, so it may take a little trial and error before you find the perfect timing for your poached eggs. I use medium eggs from the fridge and cook them for 7 minutes, which gives me the perfect runny yolk – just how I like it!

Preheat the air fryer to 180°C.

First, poach the eggs. Grease two small ramekins with spray oil and add 4 tablespoons of boiling water to each one. Crack an egg into each ramekin and cook for 7 minutes at 180°C for a runny centre. If your eggs aren't looking cooked enough, simply add a little more boiling water and cook for a further minute or so. Once cooked, carefully remove from the ramekins and set aside.

Cook the bacon in the air fryer at 180°C for 6–7 minutes or until cooked to your liking, flipping halfway through the cooking time.

Meanwhile, make the hollandaise sauce. In a blender or a bowl using a handheld blender, blitz together the egg yolks, lemon juice and a pinch of cayenne pepper. In another bowl, add the butter and microwave for 1 minute or until very hot (it's important the butter is hot and not just melted).

Slowly add the hot butter to the egg mixture while the blender is running; this will create the hollandaise sauce. If it curdles at all, just add a splash of boiling water to mixture to bring it back to a smooth consistency.

Toast the muffins in the air fryer for 1 minute (or use a toaster). Place the bacon (or ham) on the muffins, then balance the poached eggs on top. Drizzle over the hollandaise sauce to serve.

BACON, HALLOUMI AND AVOCADO STACK

A brunch fit for a king (or queen), this will definitely set you up for the day. The combination of bacon, halloumi and avocado is amazing. If you don't have any sourdough bread, it's equally delicious on a toasted bagel too.

△ Cooking time: 15 minutes

⊜ Preparation time: 5 minutes

♡ Calories: 502 kcals per serving

For the stack

3 smoked streaky bacon rashers

50g halloumi

8 cherry tomatoes on the vine

50g avocado

A pinch of chilli flakes

Squeeze of fresh lemon or 1 teaspoon fresh lemon juice

1 thick-cut slice of sourdough bread (or your favourite bread)

1 teaspoon chilli jam (see page 208 for homemade)

Preheat the air fryer to 180°C.

Add the bacon and halloumi to the air fryer and cook at 180°C for 6–7 minutes or until cooked, flipping halfway through the cooking time.

After flipping the bacon and halloumi, add the cherry tomatoes to the air fryer and cook for 3 minutes.

Meanwhile, smash your avocado, add a pinch each of salt, pepper and the chilli flakes, then stir in the lemon juice.

Toast the sourdough bread in the air fryer for 5 minutes at 180°C, turning halfway through the cooking time.

Spread the toasted sourdough with the smashed avocado, then add the bacon and halloumi. Drizzle over some chilli jam, then stack the tomatoes on top.

CHEESY OMELETTE

SERVES
1

Air-fryer omelettes are just so easy to make. For the filling, feel free to add whatever ingredients you have to use up in your fridge! This recipe makes enough for one, but you can easily double it to make a sharing size omelette.

Cooking time: 10 minutes

Preparation time: 5 minutes

Calories: 527 kcals per serving

For the omelette

3 eggs

¼ red pepper, chopped

2 spring onions, sliced

6 cherry tomatoes, halved

50g sweetcorn kernels

2 thick-cut ham slices, chopped

30g Cheddar cheese, grated

Non-stick spray oil

In a bowl, whisk together the eggs and season with a pinch of salt and pepper. Add the red pepper, spring onions, cherry tomatoes, sweetcorn kernels and ham.

Line the air fryer and spray with non-stick spray oil. Pour the egg mixture into the air fryer, top with the grated cheese and cook at 180°C for 10 minutes or until cooked to your liking.

SHAKSHUKA WITH CHORIZO AND FETA

This is an excellent, easy breakfast; it's just dreamy with a slice of sourdough bread to dunk. Be sure to warm through the chopped tomatoes first to get them hot, this helps to cook the egg and should ensure a deliciously runny yolk.

 Cooking time: 10 minutes

 Preparation time: 5 minutes

Calories: 467 kcals per serving

For the shakshuka

½ x 400-g can of chopped tomatoes with herbs

½ teaspoon garlic paste

½ teaspoon dried oregano

A pinch of chilli flakes

1 egg

15g diced chorizo

15g feta

To serve

1 slice of sourdough bread (or your choice of bread)

Preheat the air fryer to 180°C.

Add the tomatoes to a microwave-safe bowl, mix in the garlic paste, oregano and a pinch of chilli flakes, season with salt and pepper. Warm the tomatoes in the microwave for about 2 minutes, making sure they are piping hot.

In an individual air fryer-safe dish, add the hot tomatoes. Make a space in the middle of the tomatoes and crack in the egg, now scatter over the chorizo and crumble over the feta.

Bake in the air fryer at 180°C for 6–7 minutes or until the egg has set but the yolk is still runny.

Halfway through the cooking time, add the bread to toast (or use a toaster). Serve up and enjoy!

BREAKFAST BURRITOS

There's something so glorious about a breakfast burrito. You can easily adapt these by adding your favourite breakfast fillings.

Cooking time: 20 minutes

Preparation time: 5 minutes

Calories: 509 kcals per serving

For the burritos

2 hash browns

2 eggs

40g Cheddar cheese, grated

4 bacon medallions

50g avocado, diced

6 cherry tomatoes, diced

2 tablespoons hot sauce or chilli jam (see page 208 for homemade)

2 tortilla wraps

Non-stick spray oil

To serve

Your choice of ketchup or sauce

Preheat the air fryer to 180°C.

Add the hash browns to the air fryer and cook at 180°C for 8 minutes, flipping halfway through the cooking time.

Whisk the eggs and season with a pinch of salt and pepper. Add the egg mixture to a buttered air fryer-safe dish and cook at 180°C for 4 minutes, or until the egg has set.

Add the cooked hash browns, eggs, cheese, bacon, avocado, diced tomatoes, salt and pepper and your choice of hot sauce or chilli jam to the wraps and fold tightly.

Spray the air fryer with non-stick spray oil.

Place the burritos seam side down in the air fryer, brush with a little oil and cook at 180°C for 7–8 minutes, or until crispy and golden on the outside.

Slice in half and serve.

ULTIMATE BREAKFAST BURGER

SERVES 1

This truly is heaven in a brioche bun!

- Cooking time: 15 minutes
- Preparation time: 5 minutes
- Calories: 495 kcals per serving

For the burger

2 reduced fat pork sausages

2 smoked streaky bacon rashers

1 egg

Non-stick spray oil

To serve

1 brioche bun, sliced

A handful of rocket

1 tablespoon chilli jam (see page 208 for homemade)

Line the air fryer and preheat to 180°C.

Remove the skins from the sausages and form the sausagemeat into a round patty.

Add the patty to the air fryer and cook at 180°C for 6 minutes.

After 6 minutes, flip the sausage patty over. Add in the bacon and cook for 4 minutes.

After 3 minutes, flip the bacon over. Crack the egg into an egg ring or ramekin that has been sprayed with non-stick spray oil. Add to the air fryer and cook for a further 5 minutes or until the egg is cooked to your liking.

Towards the end of the cooking time, add the brioche bun to toast for a couple of minutes.

Assemble the burger by layering the sausage patty, bacon, egg and rocket. Drizzle over the chilli jam before serving.

BABY POTATO AND CHORIZO HASH

Who doesn't love a good potato hash? This one is a brilliant choice for a hearty breakfast. It's especially delicious served with a couple of fried eggs on top.

Cooking time: 20 minutes

Preparation time: 5 minutes

Calories: 225 kcals per serving

For the potato hash

400g baby potatoes

Non-stick spray oil

½ teaspoon garlic paste

½ teaspoon smoked paprika

50g chorizo, diced

½ red pepper, diced

½ onion, diced

Salt and freshly ground black pepper

To serve

1 spring onion, sliced

Sriracha mayo

Preheat the air fryer to 180°C.

Chop the baby potatoes into small, even-sized chunks, place in a bowl and coat with the non-stick spray oil. Add the garlic paste and sprinkle over the smoked paprika, salt and pepper, then shake the bowl to make sure every chunk of potato is well coated.

Place in the air fryer and cook at 180°C for 13 minutes, shaking halfway through the cooking time.

After 13 minutes, when they potatoes are nearly cooked, add the diced chorizo, red pepper and onion and cook for a further 7 minutes or until the chorizo turns crispy.

Divide the hash between two serving plates and top with the sliced spring onions and some sriracha mayo.

FULL ENGLISH TRAYBAKE

SERVES 2

You really can't beat a good (air)fry up! Save on the washing up by cooking it all together in the air fryer with this Full English traybake. I love it with a side of buttered toast and some hot tea or coffee!

⏱ Cooking time: 20 minutes

🍴 Preparation time: 5 minutes

♡ Calories: 592 kcals per serving

For the traybake

250g baby potatoes, quartered

1 teaspoon oil

4 pork chipolatas

4 smoked streaky bacon rashers (or your favourite bacon)

2 eggs

8 mushrooms

2 strings of cherry tomatoes on the vine

1 x 200-g can baked beans

To serve

Your choice of ketchup or sauce

Preheat the air fryer to 180°C.

Start by tossing the quartered baby potatoes in the oil, then season them with some salt and pepper. Place the potatoes in the air fryer and cook at 180°C for 7 minutes.

After 7 minutes, turn the potatoes, add the chipolatas and cook together at 180°C for a further 6 minutes.

Next, turn the sausages, add the bacon rashers to the air fryer and cook at 180°C for a further 3 minutes.

Turn everything over once more, then find a space for the eggs and crack them directly into the air fryer (or you can crack them into greased ramekins).

Add the mushrooms, tomatoes and beans (in a ramekin) to the air fryer and cook together at 180°C for 4 minutes or until cooked through.

CHEESY BACON AND EGG BAGEL

These bacon-wrapped bagels make a dreamy, speedy breakfast. The hole in the centre of the bagel makes the perfect well in which to crack and cook the egg.

Cooking time: 10 minutes

Preparation time: 5 minutes

Calories: 595 kcals per serving

For the bagel

1 bagel

1 tablespoon butter

4 streaky bacon rashers

2 eggs

20g Cheddar cheese, grated

To serve

Your choice of ketchup or sauce

Preheat the air fryer to 200°C.

Slice the bagel in half across the middle and then lightly butter the insides.

Wrap two of the streaky bacon rashers around each of the bagel halves, winding the rashers around the bagel and through the centre hole.

Place the bacon-wrapped bagel halves in the air fryer with the cut sides facing upwards. Cook at 200°C for 5 minutes.

Flip the bagel halves over. Crack an egg into the centre hole of each bagel half and then scatter over the grated Cheddar cheese. Cook at 200°C for a further 5 minutes or until the cheese is melted and the egg is cooked.

MELTING MIDDLE BAKED OATS

Such a delicious warm and sweet breakfast. You can also add a layer of extra chocolate chips before covering with the oats for a delicious melting middle!

Cooking time: 25 minutes

Preparation time: 5 minutes

Calories: 504 kcals per serving

For the baked oats

1 banana

100g rolled oats

2 tablespoons soft brown sugar

110ml milk

2 eggs

1 teaspoon baking soda

50g milk chocolate chips

Preheat the air fryer to 160°C.

Combine all of the ingredients, except the milk chocolate chips, in a bowl. Stir until everything is well mixed.

Gently fold the choc chips through the oat mixture. Divide the oat mixture between two heatproof ramekins.

Cook at 160°C for 25 minutes. Leave to cool for a few minutes before serving.

CHOCOLATE BANANA ROLL UP

These are great for kids and so versatile! You could add strawberries instead of bananas.

Cooking time: 7 minutes

Preparation time: 5 minutes

Calories: 525 kcals per serving

For the roll up

2 slices of brioche bread

1 tablespoon chocolate hazelnut spread

1 banana, sliced in half widthways to make two shorter pieces

1 egg

30ml milk

½ teaspoon vanilla extract

1 tablespoon granulated white sugar

½ teaspoon ground cinnamon

To serve

Fresh strawberries

Preheat the air fryer to 180°C.

Cut the crusts off the brioche bread slices and then roll out to flatten.

Spread one side of the brioche bread with the chocolate hazelnut spread, add a banana half to each slice of bread and roll up tightly around the banana.

Whisk together the egg, milk and vanilla extract in a bowl.

Dip the roll up into the egg mixture to coat, place in the air fryer and cook at 180°C for 7 minutes, turning halfway through the cooking time.

Combine the sugar and cinnamon in a small bowl. Add the cooked banana roll ups to coat.

Serve topped with fresh strawberries, and maybe a drizzle of extra melted chocolate spread.

GRANOLA YOGURT BOWL WITH BAKED FRUIT COMPOTE

SERVES 4

This granola recipe is really easy and delicious, so there's no need to buy ready made granola when you can make it at home and customise it with whatever you like! Stored in an air-tight container, the granola should last a couple of weeks.

Cooking time: 22 minutes

Preparation time: 10 minutes

Calories: 297 kcals per serving

For the granola

100g rolled oats

80g mixed nuts (such as almonds, walnuts and peanuts), roughly chopped

2 tablespoons golden syrup

1 teaspoon olive oil

For the compote

60g strawberries, hulled and halved

60g raspberries

60g blackberries

1 tablespoon honey

To serve

Greek yogurt

In a mixing bowl, combine the rolled oats, nuts, golden syrup and oil.

Line the air fryer and add the oats, pushing them down to spread them out as evenly as you can.

Air fry at 170°C for 5 minutes, take out and stir after 5 minutes to ensure everywhere gets crunchy, return to the air fryer for a further 5 minutes.

Take out and let the granola cool for at least 20 minutes, then you can break it up, leaving some chunky bits.

For the compote, place the strawberries, raspberries and blackberries in an air-fryer safe tray or heatproof dish. Drizzle the honey over the berries and cook at 180°C for 12 minutes. Once the berries are cooked, mash them with a fork, transfer to a small bowl and leave to cool in the fridge.

Serve the granola with some Greek yogurt and the baked fruit compote.

COOK'S TIP

Any dried fruits work really well in this breakfast granola – simply add them into the mixture at the very end. For extra indulgence, you could even add a few milk chocolate chips. You can also use any fresh fruit you like for the compote too, although I find mixed berries work best.

FRENCH TOAST STICKS WITH SUMMER BERRIES

SERVES
2

These are so easy to make and the whole family will love them. Use brioche bread for that extra sweetness and top with fresh berries. You can also top these with chocolate or biscuit spread, the possibilities are endless. You may need to cook these in batches, but it's worth it.

Cooking time: 6 minutes

Preparation time: 5 minutes

Calories: 364 kcals per serving

For the French toast

4 slices of brioche bread

1 egg

50ml milk

½ teaspoon vanilla extract

Non-stick spray oil

To serve

Fresh berries or fruit, such as raspberries or nectarines

2 teaspoons icing sugar

2 tablespoons golden syrup

Preheat the air fryer to 180°C.

Slice the brioche bread lengthways into four sticks.

Whisk together the eggs, milk and vanilla extract.

Dip the brioche sticks in the egg mixture, coating all sides (do this quickly so the bread doesn't turn soggy).

Line and spray the air fryer with non-stick spray oil then place the bread in, leaving space around each stick.

Air fry for 5–6 minutes at 180°C, flipping them over halfway through the cooking time.

Place the French toast sticks on a serving plate, add the fresh fruit and dust with icing sugar. Drizzle over the golden syrup immediately before serving.

BLUEBERRY MUFFINS

MAKES 4

These muffins are super easy to make. You can whip up a batch and store them in an air-tight container to enjoy throughout the week. This recipe is really versatile. Swap out the blueberries for other berries, such as raspberries with a handful of white chocolate chips.

Cooking time: 20 minutes

Preparation time: 5 minutes

Calories: 282 kcals per muffin

For the muffins

100g plain flour, sifted

75g granulated white sugar

1 teaspoon baking powder

A pinch of salt

1 egg

60ml milk

40ml sunflower oil

½ teaspoon vanilla extract

100g blueberries

Preheat the air fryer to 150°C.

In a large mixing bowl, combine the flour, sugar, baking powder and salt.

In a jug or bowl, whisk together the egg, milk, sunflower oil and vanilla extract.

Add the egg mixture to the flour mix and stir together well to combine, then fold the blueberries into the mixture.

Divide the mixture equally between 4 large paper or silicone muffin cases.

Cook at 150°C for 20 minutes.

Remove from the air fryer and leave to cool for at least 5 minutes before serving.

COOK'S TIP

This recipe makes four large muffins, but you can always double up the quantities given here to make more. Depending on the size of your air fryer, you may need to cook them in batches.

STRAWBERRY DANISH PASTRIES

MAKES
3

Buttery puff pastry filled with a jammy fruit filling, these heart-shaped sweet pastries make a tasty breakfast or special treat any time of the day.

- Cooking time: 7 minutes
- Preparation time: 5 minutes
- Calories: 175 kcals per pastry

For the pastries

1 sheet of ready-rolled puff pastry (about 320g in weight)

25g cream cheese

15g icing sugar, plus extra for dusting

3 strawberries

1 egg, beaten

2 teaspoons strawberry jam

Preheat the air fryer to 170°C.

Unroll the puff pastry sheet and cut it into 3 large heart shapes, either using a shaped cutter or freehand. Alternatively, you can cut them into squares.

Next, lightly score another smaller heart (or square) into each pastry shape, being careful not to cut all the way through the pastry.

Mix together the cream cheese and icing sugar and spread it evenly over the inner heart shapes.

Slice up the strawberries and top the cream cheese mixture with a few slices.

Brush the sides of the pastry with the beaten egg and cook for 7 minutes at 170°C.

Mix the jam with a splash of hot water and spoon the jammy mixture over the pastries.

Dust the pastries with icing sugar before serving.

CHAPTER

2

LUNCH

SPICY CHERRY TOMATO AND RED PEPPER SOUP WITH GRILLED CHEESE

This brilliant soup goes hand in hand with my oozing grilled cheese recipe. Dunk grilled cheese into your air fryer tomato and red pepper soup and you'll be in heaven. Feel free to use 'light' versions of the cheese or bread to reduce the calories a little.

Cooking time: 23 minutes

Preparation time: 10 minutes

Calories: 125 kcals per serving of soup, 433 kcal per grilled cheese

For the soup

1 red pepper

1 red onion

3 garlic cloves

600g cherry tomatoes

½ teaspoon chilli flakes

1 teaspoon dried oregano

Non-stick spray oil

400ml vegetable stock

1 tablespoon chopped fresh basil, plus extra sprigs to serve

50ml single cream

Salt and freshly ground black pepper

For the grilled cheese

2 slices bread, preferably from a fresh crusty loaf such as tiger bread

1 tablespoon 'light' mayonnaise (or butter)

2 cheese slices (I use Gouda and red Leicester)

Preheat the air fryer to 180°C.

Chop the red pepper and red onion into large chunks. Peel the garlic, but keep the cloves whole.

Line the air fryer and add the red pepper, red onion, garlic and cherry tomatoes and sprinkle over the chilli flakes and dried oregano with some salt and pepper.

Spray the ingredients in the air fryer with non-stick spray oil and air fry at 180°C for 15 minutes, shaking the tray halfway through the cooking time.

Once cooked, transfer everything to a blender or a big pan and use a handheld stick blender. Pour in the vegetable stock and chopped basil, then blitz until smooth.

Divide the soup between four bowls, drizzle over the single cream and garnish with fresh basil sprigs.

To make the grilled cheese, spread the slices of bread on one side with the mayo. With the mayo sides on the outside, make a sandwich with the two slices of cheese.

Increase the temperature of the air fryer to 190°C. Place the grilled cheese sandwich in the air fryer and cook at 190°C for 4 minutes, then flip the sandwich over and cook at 190°C for a further 4 minutes or until golden and crispy.

CHICKEN PESTO CIABATTA SANDWICH

If you follow me on Instagram, you'll probably already know how much I adore this flavour combo. It works really well in sandwiches, wraps and paninis. It's simply divine! I like to use cherry tomatoes on the vine for that extra sweetness, although they have a habit of falling out of the sandwich, but I think it's worth it.

Cooking time: 7 minutes

Preparation time: 5 minutes

Calories: 550 kcals per serving

For the sandwich

1 tablespoon 'light' mayonnaise

1 tablespoon green basil pesto

75g shredded roast chicken (see my Roast Chicken recipe on page 106)

1 ciabatta roll or 2 slices of thick-cut bread (I like to use tiger bread)

1 teaspoon butter

50g mozzarella cheese

Handful of cherry tomatoes, sliced (or use 1 larger tomato, sliced)

Handful of rocket leaves

Preheat the air fryer to 180°C.

In a bowl, mix together the mayo and pesto. Stir in the shredded roast chicken until fully coated in the pesto mayo.

Spread the roll or slices of bread on one side with the butter. With the buttered sides on the outside, make a sandwich by layering the chicken mixture, mozzarella, tomatoes and rocket. Press down slightly.

Place the sandwich in the air fryer and cook at 180°C for 7 minutes, flipping the sandwich over halfway through the cooking time. Serve straight away.

CAPRESE FOCACCIA

I love the combination of mozzarella, pesto and tomato, it's so fresh and tasty. These focaccia combine all of these flavours with the sweetness of the balsamic and the peppery rocket to finish. Simply delicious! You can buy sliced focaccia from most supermarkets now in packs of four, or you can use flatbreads, pitas or even bagels instead.

Cooking time: 8 minutes

Preparation time: 5 minutes

Calories: 487 kcals per serving

For the focaccia

2 focaccia loaves, sliced

50g green basil pesto

1 mozzarella ball, sliced into thin rounds

150g cherry tomatoes, halved

Cracked black peppercorns

To serve

1 tablespoon balsamic glaze

Handful of rocket leaves

Spread the sliced focaccia with the pesto. Add the mozzarella on top of each focaccia slice, then layer on the tomatoes and sprinkle with cracked black pepper.

Place in the air fryer and cook at 180°C for 8 minutes, or until the cheese is bubbling.

Drizzle over the balsamic glaze and scatter over the rocket leaves.

LOADED POTATO SKINS

Loaded potato skins are an American diner classic. They always remind me of going to American-themed restaurants when I was younger. Microwaving your potato first gives you a quick head start here, but if you don't have a microwave then you can bake them for around 50 minutes on 190°C, turning halfway through the cooking time, and then follow the rest of the steps.

Cooking time: 30 minutes

Preparation time: 10 minutes

Calories: 531 kcals per serving

For the potato skins

2 baking potatoes (around 250g each)

Olive oil

1 tablespoon butter

4 spring onions

6 streaky smoked bacon rashers, cooked and chopped

80g red Leicester cheese

Salt and freshly ground black pepper

To serve

1 tablespoon sour cream

1 tablespoon barbecue sauce

Pierce the potatoes with a fork, then microwave them for 10 minutes, turning halfway through the cooking time, to soften.

Once softened, rub each potato with a little olive oil and season with salt and pepper.

Place the potatoes in the air fryer and cook at 190°C for 10 minutes to crisp up the skins.

Cut the potatoes in half and scoop out the insides, putting these insides in a bowl. Add a knob of butter to the cooked potato insides along with the spring onions, bacon and half of the cheese.

Scoop the filling back into the potato skins and top with the rest of the cheese.

Return the potato skins to the air fryer and cook at 190°C for 10 minutes.

Serve with a dollop of sour cream and drizzled with the barbecue sauce.

PIZZA TOASTIES

"You can't please everybody.... You're not pizza!" This quick-and-easy idea for a delicious pizza toast went a little bit viral on my social channels when I first posted the idea. Now, I'm sharing it here too.

 Cooking time: 7 minutes

 Preparation time: 5 minutes

Calories: 304 kcals per serving

For the toasties

2 tablespoons tomato purée

½ teaspoon dried oregano

¼ teaspoon chilli flakes

½ teaspoon garlic paste

4 slices of white bread from a small loaf

2 ham slices

80g mozzarella cheese, grated

Make your pizza sauce by combining the tomato purée with the dried oregano, chilli flakes and garlic paste. Add a splash of water to loosen the sauce slightly and mix well.

Spread two of the slices of bread with the pizza sauce, then add a ham slice to each piece of bread along with half of the cheese. Spread the other slices of bread with the rest of the pizza sauce, then top with the rest of the cheese.

Place the toast in the air fryer and cook at 160°C for 7 minutes.

Slice in half and serve immediately.

SAUSAGE, BEAN AND CHEESE MINI PASTIES

I love finding inventive ways of using wraps. Pasties are a favourite comfort food of mine, and sausages, beans and cheese is a winning combo. Using wraps means that these pasties are much lighter than the usual puff pastry, but equally delicious. You can also use one large wrap instead of two small ones.

Cooking time: 20 minutes

Preparation time: 10 minutes

Calories: 415 kcals per serving

For the pasties

4 chicken sausages

4 mini wraps

1 egg, beaten

1 x 200-g can baked beans

30g 'light' Cheddar cheese, grated

Salt and freshly ground black pepper

Start by cooking the chicken sausages. They can be cooked in the air fryer at 180°C for 12 minutes (depending on the thickness of the sausages, they may need a little longer), turning halfway through the cooking time.

Once cooked, slice each of the sausages into small, bite-sized pieces.

Take a mini wrap and brush around the sides with the beaten egg. Place a spoonful of baked beans on one side only of the wrap along with the sausage pieces and grated cheese, leaving a little space around the edges. Don't overfill the wraps otherwise they won't stay closed! Season with salt and pepper.

Fold the filled wraps over to create half moon shapes, then crimp around the edges with a fork. Brush the wraps all over with the beaten egg.

Place the pasties in the air fryer and cook at 180°C for 8 minutes or until golden. Leave to cool for a few minutes before serving.

TORTILLA BURRITO BOWLS

This is such a lovely twist on the chicken burrito, combining all of those familiar Mexican fillings in a bowl made from a toasted tortilla wrap. Depending on your air fryer, you may find it best to shape your wrap into a square box rather than a rounded bowl.

Cooking time: 15 minutes

Preparation time: 10 minutes

Calories: 650 kcals per serving

For the chicken

2 chicken breasts

1 teaspoon smoked paprika

½ teaspoon cayenne pepper

½ teaspoon ground cumin

½ teaspoon garlic powder

1 teaspoon oil

Salt and freshly ground black pepper

For the tortilla burrito bowls

Non-stick spray oil

2 tortilla wraps

To serve

1 x 250-g pouch microwaveable Mexican rice (or see my recipe on page 201 for a homemade version)

1 x 250-g can sweetcorn kernels

200g cherry tomatoes, diced

1 avocado, peeled, stoned and sliced

½ red onion, sliced

2 tablespoons salsa

2 tablespoons sour cream

Fresh lime wedges, for squeezing over

Coriander sprigs

Preheat the air fryer to 180°C.

Butterfly the chicken breasts and season with the smoked paprika, cayenne pepper, ground cumin, garlic powder and salt and pepper. Drizzle over the oil, making sure the chicken is coated all over.

Place the butterflied chicken in the air fryer and cook at 180°C for 10–12 minutes or until cooked through, flipping over halfway through the cooking time.

Once cooked, slice the chicken and set aside.

Spray a heatproof bowl suitable to go in your air fryer with some non-stick spray oil. Push the tortilla into the prepared bowl to make a curved bowl shape.

Place the tortilla bowl in the air fryer and cook at 180°C for 3 minutes or until it starts to go crispy.

Once shaped and crispy, assemble your tortilla burrito bowls. Fill each bowl with the sliced chicken, Mexican rice, sweetcorn kernels, cherry tomatoes and avocado. Top with the red onion slices, salsa and sour cream. Squeeze over the lime and garnish with coriander sprigs.

STICKY SALMON WITH MANGO SALSA

This delicious salmon recipe comes together in under 30 minutes. It's great with either a crisp green salad, some boiled new potatoes or plain steamed rice.

- Cooking time: 10 minutes
- Preparation time: 15 minutes
- Calories: 462 kcals per serving

For the salmon

2 salmon fillets

1 tablespoon soy sauce

1 tablespoon honey

1 tablespoon sweet chilli sauce

1 teaspoon garlic paste

½ teaspoon chilli flakes

Salt and freshly ground black pepper

Non-stick spray oil

For the salsa

1 mango, peeled, stoned and diced

1 red pepper, deseeded and diced

1 avocado, peeled, stoned and diced

½ red onion, diced

Juice of 1 lime

1 tablespoon chopped coriander

Salt and freshly ground black pepper

To serve

Crisp green salad

First, prepare the salmon. Season the salmon fillets with salt and pepper. Mix together the soy, honey, sweet chilli sauce, garlic paste and chilli flakes. Pour over the salmon to coat, then marinate in the fridge for at least 10 minutes or up to an hour.

Next, make the salsa. Combine the diced mango, red pepper, avocado and red onion in a bowl. Season with a pinch each of salt and pepper, then squeeze over the lime juice and top with the chopped coriander. Set aside in the fridge.

When ready to cook, preheat the air fryer to 180°C.

Spray the air fryer with non-stick spray oil. Add the salmon fillets and cook at 180°C for 10 minutes, or until cooked through.

Serve the salmon with the chilled mango salsa and a crisp green salad.

GOATS' CHEESE, BEETROOT AND CARAMELISED ONION TARTS

Goats' cheese, beetroot and caramelised onion are three of my favourite flavours, and happily they all work together beautifully. The flaky, buttery puff pastry makes the perfect base for these simple tarts.

Cooking time: 15 minutes per tart

Preparation time: 5 minutes

Calories: 514 kcals per serving

For the tarts

1 sheet of ready-rolled puff pastry (about 320g in weight)

4 tablespoons caramelised onion chutney

4 cooked beetroot in natural juices (not in vinegar)

80g goats' cheese, crumbled

To serve

Handful of walnuts, roughly chopped

Handful of rocket leaves

Balsamic glaze (optional)

Preheat the air fryer to 180°C.

Unroll the puff pastry sheet, but keep it on its parchment paper. Cut the pastry into 4 equal-sized pieces.

Depending on the size of your air fryer, you may be able to cook more than one tart at a time. If not, work in batches.

Place the puff pastry in the air fryer and cook at 180°C for around 10 minutes or until puffed up and golden.

Once cooked, remove the puff pastry from the air fryer and, using the back of a spoon, flatten the inside of the pastry, leaving a border all the way round.

Spread the caramelised onion chutney over the flattened area. Thinly slice the beetroot and lay it over the chutney, then sprinkle over the goats' cheese.

Place the tart in the air fryer and cook at 180°C for a further 5 minutes.

Scatter over some chopped walnuts and few rocket leaves. Drizzle with a little balsamic glaze, if using, before serving.

CRISPY CHICKEN CAESAR SALAD

SERVES
2

This crispy chicken salad is my take on the classic Caesar salad, but with a delicious twist.

Cooking time: 16 minutes

Preparation time: 10 minutes

Calories: 585 kcals per serving

For the chicken

2 chicken breasts

20g plain flour

1 egg

40g panko breadcrumbs

½ teaspoon dried oregano

Salt and freshly ground black pepper

Non-stick spray oil

For the salad

4 bacon rashers

1 Romaine lettuce, separated into leaves

2 soft-boiled eggs, peeled and quartered

12 cherry tomatoes, halved

20g Parmesan cheese shavings

For the dressing

2 tablespoons 'light' mayonnaise

1 teaspoon lemon juice

1 teaspoon Worcestershire sauce

1 teaspoon Dijon mustard

½ teaspoon garlic paste

10g Parmesan cheese, grated

Preheat the air fryer to 180°C.

First, prepare the chicken. Butterfly the chicken breasts, then season them with salt and pepper.

Organise your breading station by placing the flour in a shallow bowl and season with salt and pepper. In a second bowl, beat the egg. In a third bowl, combine the panko breadcrumbs with the dried oregano, and season with a little salt and pepper.

Coat the butterflied chicken first in the flour, then dip it into the beaten egg and finally into the panko breadcrumbs, making sure it is fully coated.

Place the breadcrumbed chicken in the air fryer and spray with non-stick spray oil. Cook at 180°C for 10 minutes. After 10 minutes, flip the chicken over, add the bacon rashers and cook for a further 6 minutes, turning the bacon after 3 minutes of the cooking time.

Once the chicken and bacon are cooked, slice them into thin strips.

Meanwhile, make the dressing. Combine the mayonnaise, lemon juice, Worcestershire sauce, Dijon mustard, garlic paste and grated Parmesan cheese in a bowl or jug. Thin the dressing with a splash of water, if necessary.

Layer the lettuce leaves in a salad bowl. Add the crispy chicken slices and bacon strips, boiled eggs and cherry tomatoes. Drizzle the dressing over the salad and top with the shavings of Parmesan cheese.

CHEESY COUSCOUS STUFFED PEPPERS

This is a really delicious light lunch. I love the sweetness of red peppers, which roast so well in the air fryer. The couscous filling is really quick to put together, making this dish a great veggie option.

Cooking time: 18 minutes

Preparation time: 10 minutes

Calories: 340 kcals per serving

For the peppers

2 red or yellow peppers

Non-stick spray oil

Salt and freshly ground black pepper

For the couscous filling

80g couscous

100ml hot vegetable stock (or 100ml boiling water mixed with ½ vegetable stock pot)

6 cherry tomatoes, diced

2 spring onions, sliced

½ teaspoon turmeric

½ teaspoon paprika

Salt and freshly ground black pepper

For the tomato sauce

½ x 400-g can chopped tomatoes with herbs

1 teaspoon garlic paste

½ teaspoon dried oregano

50g Cheddar cheese (or mozzarella), grated

Salt and freshly ground black pepper

Slice the red or yellow peppers in half vertically down the middle. You can keep the stalks on for decoration, but remove the ribs and seeds.

Place the pepper halves in the air fryer, spray with oil and season with salt and pepper, then cook at 180°C for 10 minutes.

Meanwhile, place the couscous in a heatproof bowl. Pour over the hot vegetable stock, cover the bowl and leave for 5 minutes.

Once the couscous is ready, fluff up the grains with a fork, then mix in the cherry tomatoes, spring onions, turmeric and paprika. Season with a pinch each of salt and pepper.

Mix the chopped tomatoes with a little garlic paste and season with a sprinkle of dried oregano, salt and pepper. Warm in the microwave for 2 minutes or until hot.

Spread the tomato sauce over the base of a roasting tray (or take out the air fryer tray and spread the tomato mixture over the base).

Fill the pepper halves with the couscous, nestle them into the tomato sauce and scatter over the grated cheese.

Place the roasting tray in the air fryer and cook at 180°C for 6 minutes or until bubbling and golden.

CURRIED CAULIFLOWER SOUP

SERVES 4

The air fryer is so versatile, you can even use it to make the most delicious soups! Serve this roasted, curried cauliflower soup with homemade croutons.

Cooking time: 26 minutes

Preparation time: 10 minutes

Calories: 184 kcals per serving

For the soup

1 head of cauliflower

2 celery stalks

1 leek

Non-stick spray oil

50ml single cream

1 tablespoon medium curry powder

700ml hot vegetable stock

Salt and freshly ground black pepper

For the croutons

4 slices of white bread, cut into small cubes (you can use up stale bread)

1 tablespoon melted butter

½ teaspoon garlic paste

½ teaspoon dried parsley

Salt and freshly ground black pepper

Separate the cauliflower into small florets. Slice the celery and leek into thin rounds.

Preheat the air fryer to 180°C.

Line the air fryer and add the cauliflower florets, celery and leek slices. Spray with oil and season with salt and pepper. Cook at 180°C for 15 minutes, or until the vegetables have softened and are starting to brown.

Transfer the cooked veg to a blender and add the cream and curry powder. Blitz until smooth.

Add the hot vegetable stock and blitz again. Keep warm while you make the croutons.

To make the croutons, toss the cubes of bread in a mixture of melted butter, garlic paste, dried parsley and a pinch each of salt and pepper.

Place the croutons in the air fryer and cook at 180°C for 6 minutes or until crispy, turning halfway through cooking.

Divide the soup between individual bowls and scatter the croutons over the top before serving.

SPRING ROLL NOODLE BOWL

SERVES
2

This Asian-inspired noodle bowl is full of flavour and goodness with veggie-filled spring rolls nestled on top. If you like things extra spicy, add a pinch of chilli flakes to the broth or drizzle over some sriracha.

Cooking time: 16 minutes

Preparation time: 15 minutes

Calories: 376 kcals per serving

For the spring rolls

1 carrot, very finely sliced

4 spring onions, very finely sliced

100g red cabbage, very finely sliced

30g mushrooms, finely chopped

1 teaspoon garlic paste

1 teaspoon ginger paste

1½ tablespoons dark soy sauce

6 sheets of rice paper or spring roll wrappers

Freshly ground black pepper

Non-stick spray oil

For the noodle bowl

1 pak choi, quartered

400ml boiling water

1 vegetable stock cube

1 lemongrass stalk

2 nests of fine rice noodles (or use straight-to-wok noodles)

For the peanut sauce

1 tablespoon peanut butter (crunchy or smooth)

1 tablespoon dark soy sauce

Add all of the veggies to a bowl with the garlic paste, ginger paste, ½ tablespoon of the soy sauce and a pinch of black pepper. Mix well and leave to marinate for 30 minutes.

Soak the sheets of rice paper in cold water for a few seconds.

One by one, add some of the veggie mixture to the centre of each rice paper sheet, fold in the sides and then roll up to make a spring roll. Repeat until all the rice paper sheets and veggies are used up.

Place the spring rolls in the air fryer. Spray with spray oil and cook at 180°C for 14 minutes or until crispy, turning halfway through the cooking time.

Remove the spring rolls from the air fryer and set aside. Add the pak choi to gently cook at 180°C for 2 minutes.

Mix together the boiling water and the stock cube in a jug. Add 1 tablespoon of soy sauce and the lemongrass stalk.

When ready to serve, place a noodle nest in each bowl. Pour over the hot stock to 'cook' the noodles following the instructions on the packet.

Meanwhile, to make the quick peanut sauce, combine all the ingredients in a small bowl with 1 tablespoon water until smooth. Add a splash more water to thin the sauce, if needed.

Add the pak choi quarters to the bowls of noodles, and then rest the crispy spring rolls on top. Serve with a drizzle of the peanut sauce.

CREAMY GARLIC MUSHROOMS ON TOAST

SERVES 1

These mushrooms work so well in the air fryer and take no time at all. A delicious veggie lunch or even breakfast.

Cooking time: 13 minutes

Preparation time: 2 minutes

Calories: 238 kcals per serving

For the mushrooms

100g mushrooms (use any type you like, baby button mushrooms work really well), sliced in half if large

1 teaspoon butter

½ teaspoon garlic paste

35g 'light' cream cheese

Salt and freshly ground black pepper

To serve

1 slice of sourdough toast

Handful of chopped chives (optional)

Add a roasting tray or heatproof dish to the air fryer or just take out the crisper plate and cook the mushrooms in the bottom of the air fryer.

Add the mushrooms, butter, garlic paste and a pinch each of salt and pepper to the air fryer and cook at 200°C for 2 minutes.

After 2 minutes, give the mushrooms a good stir to make sure they are all coated in the butter and garlic. Cook for a further 5 minutes.

Add the cream cheese, stir everything together and let the cream cheese melt into the mushrooms. Cook for a further 1 minute. If the sauce looks a little too thick, add a splash of water.

You can toast the sourdough in the air fryer by cooking it at 200°C for 5 minutes, flipping the bread halfway through the cooking time.

Pile the creamy garlic mushrooms on top of the slice of toast, then scatter over the chopped chives, if using.

HALLOUMI SALAD WITH HONEY-MUSTARD DRESSING

SERVES
2

The combination of grilled halloumi and pomegranate seeds with this sweet and tangy dressing simply screams summer. This is a really nice veggie salad but would also be delicious with chicken.

Cooking time: 6 minutes

Preparation time: 5 minutes

Calories: 519 kcals per serving

For the halloumi

225g halloumi

1 tablespoon runny honey

¼ teaspoon chilli flakes

For the salad

80g rocket leaves

100g cucumber, sliced

80g cherry tomatoes, sliced

½ red onion, finely diced

50g pomegranate seeds

For the dressing

1 teaspoon wholegrain mustard

1 tablespoon olive oil

1 tablespoon runny honey

Slice the halloumi into small, bite-sized chunks.

Place the halloumi chunks in bowl, add the runny honey and chilli flakes and toss everything together until the halloumi is well coated.

Preheat the air fryer to 180°C.

Place the halloumi chunks in the air fryer, leaving space between the pieces if there's enough room, and cook at 180°C for 6 minutes or until golden, turning halfway through the cooking time.

To make the dressing, combine the wholegrain mustard, olive oil and runny honey in a small bowl.

When ready to serve, divide the rocket leaves between two bowls, then add the cucumber, cherry tomatoes and red onion.

Scatter the cooked halloumi on top of the salad, then sprinkle on the pomegranate seeds and drizzle over the dressing.

TUNA CRUNCH WRAP

I love making tuna crunch wraps as an alternative to a standard sandwich. The peppers and onions really jazz up the tuna along with the delicious melted cheese, and the addition of the tortilla chips gives that unexpected crunch.

Cooking time: 8 minutes

Preparation time: 10 minutes

Calories: 513 kcals per serving

For the wrap

1 x 100-g can tuna, drained

60g sweetcorn kernels

½ red pepper, finely diced

½ small red onion, finely diced

4 tablespoons 'light' mayonnaise

2 large tortilla wraps

2 mini tortilla wraps (or cut two smaller circles from one large wrap)

20g spicy tortilla chips (or your favourite flavour), roughly crushed

60g mozzarella cheese, grated

Non-stick spray oil

Salt and freshly ground black pepper

Mix together the tuna, sweetcorn, red pepper, red onion and mayo in a bowl. Season with a pinch each of salt and pepper, or to taste.

Spoon the tuna mixture into the centre of the large tortilla wraps. Cover the filling with the tortilla chips and scatter over the grated mozzarella.

Place the smaller wraps or cut-out circles on the top of the filling.

Fold the edges of the large wraps over to enclose the filling.

Place the wraps, seam side facing down, in the air fryer, spray them with a little oil and then brush it all over each wrap. Cook at 180°C for 8 minutes or until golden, turning the wraps halfway during the cooking time and adding a little more oil, if necessary.

Slice in half and allow to cool for a moment before tucking in.

FISH FINGER SANDWICH WITH TARTARE SAUCE

SERVES
2

The fish finger sandwich is just a classic, isn't it? For me, the tartare sauce is non-negotiable, but these sarnies are just as delicious with a few mushy peas instead of crisp salad leaves.

Cooking time: 15 minutes

Preparation time: 10 minutes

Calories: 580 kcals per serving

For the fish fingers

250g firm white fish fillets (such as cod or haddock)

2 tablespoons plain flour

1 egg, beaten

80g golden breadcrumbs

½ teaspoon paprika

Salt and freshly ground black pepper

For the sandwich

4 slices of thick-cut bread

2 tablespoons tartare sauce

Crisp green lettuce leaves

Pickled gherkins, sliced

Preheat the air fryer to 180°C.

Cut the fish fillets into 8 strips.

Set up three separate shallow bowls. Place the flour in the first bowl, the beaten egg in the second, and mix the breadcrumbs and paprika, seasoned with salt and pepper, in the third.

Dip each fish finger into the flour, coating it completely. Shake off any excess flour, then dip it into the beaten egg, allowing any excess to drip off. Finally, coat the fish finger in the breadcrumb mixture, pressing down gently.

Place the breaded fish fingers in the air fryer and cook at 180°C for 15 minutes or until golden and cooked through, turning halfway through the cooking time.

If you prefer the bread for your sandwich to be toasted, add the slices of bread to the air fryer (or use a toaster) towards the end of the cooking time.

To assemble the sandwiches, spread tartare sauce over the slices of bread and top with the fish fingers, then add the lettuce leaves and gherkins.

Cut each sandwich in half before serving straight away.

FALAFEL POCKET PITAS

SERVES 1

I love the Middle-Eastern flavours of falafel. These pitas are really easy to pull together and make a tasty lunch. Sometimes I spread the insides of the pocket pitas with hummus instead of yogurt because I can't decide which one I prefer.

Cooking time: 18 minutes

Preparation time: 15 minutes

Calories: 502 kcals per serving

For the falafels

1 x 400-g can chickpeas, drained and dried

½ red pepper, very finely diced

2 spring onions, very finely chopped

1 green chilli, very finely diced

1 teaspoon ground cumin

½ teaspoon paprika

½ teaspoon ground coriander

1 teaspoon garlic paste

Handful of chopped parsley

1 egg

1 tablespoon plain flour

Salt and freshly ground black pepper

Non-stick spray oil

For the pitas

2 pita breads

Salad of chopped lettuce, cucumber, red onion and tomato

2 tablespoons yogurt

2 tablespoons chilli sauce

Preheat the air fryer to 180°C.

To make the falafels, place the chickpeas in a bowl or pan and mash well with a fork or potato masher until broken down, then add the rest of the ingredients with a pinch each of salt and pepper and mix well.

Roll the falafel mixture into 8 equal-sized balls.

Place the falafel in the air fryer and spray with oil. Cook at 180°C for 18 minutes or until crispy and golden, turning halfway through the cooking time.

Meanwhile, toast the pita breads.

Once ready to serve, fill the toasted pitas with the salad and cooked falafel, then drizzle over the yogurt and chilli sauce.

CHAPTER

3

DINNER

CREAMY CHORIZO GNOCCHI BAKE

This gnocchi bake is absolutely yummy and so easy to make. Feel free to use green basil pesto instead of sundried tomato or red pepper pesto, if you prefer. And similarly you can also use your favourite soft cheese. I love one with the added flavours or garlic and herbs.

Cooking time: 11 minutes

Preparation time: 5 minutes

Calories: 520 kcals per serving

For the gnocchi

400g gnocchi

Non-stick spray oil

40g chorizo, sliced

150g cherry tomatoes

60g garlic and herb soft cheese

1 tablespoon red pesto

½ teaspoon chilli flakes

To serve

Handful of rocket leaves

Take the crisper plate out of the air fryer and preheat it to 180°C.

Either line the air fryer or just use the base.

Place the gnocchi in the air fryer, spray with non-stick spray oil and cook at 180°C for 5 minutes or until the gnocchi is starting to turn golden.

After 5 minutes, shake the gnocchi, scatter in the chorizo and cherry tomatoes, then cook for a further 3 minutes or until the chorizo starts to crisp up.

Next, unwrap the soft cheese and place it in the middle of the tray. Dot over the pesto and sprinkle in the chilli flakes, then cook everything for a further 3 minutes.

Once cooked, stir everything together. If it seems a little too thick, add a splash of water to loosen the sauce.

Divide the gnocchi between two bowls and serve with the rocket leaves on top.

HUNTER'S CHICKEN TRAYBAKE

SERVES
2

This is an absolute air-fryer wonder. I'm a big fan of hunter's chicken; it's the perfect dinner for those busy midweek nights. This dish goes great with some fresh garden peas on the side and even some extra barbecue sauce for dipping.

Cooking time: 23 minutes

Preparation time: 10 minutes

Calories: 549 kcals per serving

For the traybake

350g baby potatoes, halved

Non-stick spray oil

2 chicken breasts

1 teaspoon smoked paprika

2 bacon medallions

½ red pepper, chopped

½ yellow pepper, chopped

4 tablespoons barbecue sauce

60g mozzarella and Cheddar cheese, grated

Salt and freshly ground black pepper

Preheat the air fryer to 180°C.

Line the air fryer and then add in the baby potatoes. Season with salt and pepper, then spray with spray oil.

Season the chicken breasts with a pinch each of salt and pepper, the paprika and spray with a little more oil.

Make a space in between the potatoes and nestle in the chicken breasts. Cook at 180°C for 10 minutes.

After 10 minutes, lay a bacon rasher over each chicken breast and cook at 180°C for a further 8 minutes.

Next, add the red and yellow peppers around the chicken and on top of the potatoes.

Spread the barbecue sauce onto the bacon-wrapped chicken and sprinkle over the grated cheeses. Cook for a further 5 minutes to soften the peppers and melt the cheeses.

AUBERGINE PARMIGIANA

SERVES
2

In my opinion, the aubergine is an underrated vegetable. Smothered in tomato sauce and topped with stringy mozzarella, salty Parmesan and crunchy breadcrumbs, they make the perfect light dinner for two or a starter for four.

Cooking time: 18 minutes

Preparation time: 5 minutes

Calories: 382 kcals per serving

For the aubergines

2 aubergines, halved lengthways

1 teaspoon oil

1 x 300-g jar tomato-based sauce (or see my recipe for Marinara Sauce on page 207)

100g mozzarella, grated

30g Parmesan cheese, grated

2 tablespoons golden breadcrumbs

Salt and freshly ground black pepper

To serve

Crisp green salad

Preheat the air fryer to 180°C.

Score the cut sides of aubergines with a criss-cross pattern, rub these scored sides with a little oil and then season with salt and pepper.

Place the aubergines in the air fryer, scored side up, and cook at 180°C for 12 minutes.

Next, pour the tomato sauce over the aubergines, scatter over the grated cheeses and top with the breadcrumbs. Cook at 180°C for a further 6 minutes or until the cheese is melted and golden.

Serve the aubergine parmigiana straight away with a crisp green salad on the side.

GLAZED GAMMON

SERVES 4

Gammon is amazing when cooked in the air fryer! I love it in sandwiches or as part of a buffet, but probably my favourite way to eat gammon is with pineapple rings, a fried egg, chunky chips and garden peas – proper comfort food.

Cooking time: 40 minutes

Preparation time: 2 minutes

Calories: 232 kcals per serving

For the gammon

1 small unsmoked gammon joint (around 750g in weight)

2 tablespoons runny honey

2 tablespoons barbecue sauce

To serve

Grilled pineapple rings

Fried eggs

Chunky Chips (see page 202)

Garden peas

Preheat the air fryer to 180°C.

Place the gammon joint in the air fryer and cook at 180°C for 20 minutes. (If you're using a large gammon joint, give it an extra 10 minutes.)

After 20 minutes, turn the gammon joint over and cook at 180°C for a further 15 minutes. (Again, if you're gammon joint is large, then give it an extra 10 minutes.)

Combine the honey and barbecue sauce, then smother the outside of the meat in the glaze. Cook at 180°C for a further 5 minutes.

Allow the gammon joint to rest for a few minutes before slicing and serving with grilled pineapple rings, fried eggs, chunky chips and garden peas.

COOK'S TIP

You can switch up the flavours of the glaze that's poured over the gammon. Instead of barbecue sauce, using sweet chilli sauce works well. Or try honey mixed with wholegrain mustard.

TOAD IN THE HOLE

Sizzling sausages cooked in a batter pudding are nothing less than delicious –
especially when served with mashed potato, steamed veggies and thick gravy.
You could also divide the sausages and batter evenly between two smaller
heatproof dishes to make individual portions.

Cooking time: 27 minutes

Preparation time: 10 minutes

Calories: 454 kcals per serving

For the toad in the hole

2 eggs

100ml semi-skimmed milk

50g plain flour

2 teaspoons sunflower oil

4 thick pork sausages

Salt and freshly ground black pepper

First, make the batter. Combine the eggs, milk and flour,
whisking until smooth and to remove any lumps. Season
with a pinch each of salt and pepper. Leave the batter to
rest for at least 30 minutes (or you can leave it overnight).

Preheat the air fryer to 180°C.

Place a foil tray or a cake tin that fits into the air fryer.
Add the oil and sausages to the tray and cook at 180°C
for about 7 minutes or until starting to brown.

Once the sausages are cooked, pour over the batter. It
should sizzle! Cook at 180°C for around 20 minutes or
until the batter is crisp and golden.

STICKY SAUSAGE TRAYBAKE

SERVES
2

You've got to love a sausage traybake. It takes less than 30 minutes to make, then you just serve the dish straight up and there's minimal washing up afterwards. It's truly the perfect midweek meal.

Cooking time: 25 minutes

Preparation time: 10 minutes

Calories: 543 kcals per serving

For the traybake

350g baby potatoes, chopped into bite-sized chunks

Non-stick spray oil

8 pork chipolatas

1 red onion, sliced into strips

½ red pepper, sliced into strips

½ yellow pepper, sliced into strips

150g asparagus spears, sliced

150g cherry tomatoes

1 tablespoon runny honey

1 teaspoon garlic paste

Pinch of dried thyme

Salt and freshly ground black pepper

Preheat the air fryer to 180°C.

Line the air fryer and add the baby potato chunks. Spray generously with spray oil and cook at 180°C for 10 minutes or until nearly cooked through, turning the potatoes halfway through the cooking time.

Next, add the sausages to the air fryer and cook for a further 8 minutes, turning the sausages halfway through the cooking time.

Meanwhile, place the vegetables in a bowl, drizzle over the honey and add the garlic paste. Spray with a few pumps of spray oil and then add a pinch each of salt, pepper and dried thyme. Mix well.

Place the vegetables in the air fryer. Give everything a good mix and cook it all together for a further 7 minutes or until cooked through.

COOK'S TIP

This traybake is great with chicken sausages instead of pork chipolatas. You can also, swap out any of the veg for Tenderstem broccoli or courgettes.

LAMB KOFTA WRAPS

SERVES
4

These subtly spiced lamb koftas are so tasty. They're great served in flatbreads with strips of red onion, wedges of ripe tomato, some crumbed feta cheese and a good helping of garlic yogurt sauce.

Cooking time: 13 minutes

Preparation time: 15 minutes

Calories: 573 kcals per serving

For the koftas

500g lamb mince (10% fat)

1 onion, very finely diced

3 garlic cloves, crushed

1 teaspoon ground cumin

1 teaspoon ground coriander

1 teaspoon chilli flakes

1 teaspoon paprika

1 teaspoon cayenne pepper

Handful of chopped fresh parsley

1 egg

2 tablespoons panko breadcrumbs

Non-stick spray oil

For the garlic yogurt sauce

4 tablespoons Greek yogurt

1 garlic clove, minced

Juice of ½ lemon

1 tablespoon chopped fresh parsley

To serve

4 flatbreads

1 red onion, thinly sliced

12 cherry tomatoes, cut into wedges

80g feta cheese, crumbled

To make the koftas, place the lamb mince in a bowl. Add the onion, garlic, ground cumin, ground coriander, chilli flakes, paprika, cayenne pepper, chopped parsley, egg and breadcrumbs and mix together well. Form the lamb mixture into 8 kofta shapes.

Preheat the air fryer to 180°C.

Place the koftas in the air fryer. Spray with non-stick spray oil and cook at 180°C for 12 minutes or until golden, turning the kofta halfway through the cooking time.

To make the garlic yogurt sauce, combine the yogurt with the garlic, lemon juice and chopped parsley.

Warm the wraps in the air fryer for 1 minute.

Spread the garlic yogurt sauce over one half of each wrap, then add the koftas, red onion slices, tomato wedges and crumbled feta. Fold over the wraps before serving.

SMOKY CHIPOTLE CHICKEN FAJITAS

SERVES
4

These spicy chicken fajitas are smoky from the chipotle and with a hint of sweetness from the red onion and red and yellow peppers.

Cooking time: 23 minutes

Preparation time: 10 minutes

Calories: 565 kcals per serving

For the chicken

4 chicken breasts (around 600g in weight)

1 red pepper

1 yellow pepper

1 red onion

1 tablespoon olive oil

1 tablespoon chipotle paste

1 teaspoon smoked paprika

½ teaspoon cayenne pepper

1 teaspoon garlic paste

Salt and freshly ground black pepper

To serve

8 tortilla wraps

100g sour cream

100g salsa

80g 'light' Cheddar cheese, grated

Slice the chicken breasts into thin strips. Slice the red and yellow peppers and the red onion into thin strips that are roughly the same size as the chicken pieces.

Place the chicken, peppers and onion in a bowl, drizzle over the oil, add the chipotle paste, smoked paprika, cayenne pepper and garlic paste. Mix everything together well. Season with salt and pepper.

Line the air fryer.

Place the chicken and vegetables in the air fryer and cook at 190°C for 20 minutes or until the chicken is cooked through, shaking the tray a few times to make sure that everything cooks evenly.

Warm the tortilla wraps for around 30 seconds in the microwave or wrap them in foil and warm them in the air fryer for 3 minutes.

Fill the wraps with the spicy chicken and vegetables, then top with sour cream, salsa and grated cheese.

FISH AND CHIPS

An iconic British dish, you just can't beat a plate of fish and chips. When cooking the fish, be generous with the spray oil to ensure that the breadcrumb coating is nice and crisp.

⏲ Cooking time: 18 minutes

🥣 Preparation time: 15 minutes

♡ Calories: 349 kcals per serving

For the fish

2 cod fillets (around 150g in weight)

1 tablespoon plain flour

1 teaspoon paprika

1 teaspoon garlic powder

1 egg

50g panko breadcrumbs

Salt and freshly ground black pepper

Non-stick spray oil

For the tartare sauce

3 tablespoons 'light' mayonnaise

1 tablespoon finely diced pickled gherkin

1 tablespoon finely diced capers

1 teaspoon Dijon mustard

1 tablespoon lemon juice

1 tablespoon chopped dill or parsley

To serve

Chunky Chips (see page 202)

Mushy peas

Tomato ketchup

If the cod fillets are frozen, make sure they are fully defrosted before cooking.

Pat dry the fish, sprinkle over some salt and leave for 10 minutes while you prepare everything else. (This will take out any extra moisture from the fish.)

Preheat the air fryer to 180°C.

Prepare the chunky chips following the recipe on page 202.

To prepare the fish, combine the flour, paprika and garlic powder in a bowl with some salt and pepper. In another bowl, whisk the egg. In a third bowl, combine the panko breadcrumbs with some salt and pepper.

Coat each fish fillet first in the flour mixture. Next, dip the fish in the beaten egg and then finish by coating it in the seasoned panko breadcrumbs. Lightly press the breadcrumbs to ensure the fish is fully coated.

After the chips have been cooking for 8 minutes, add the breadcrumbed fish fillets to the air fryer, spray generously with non-stick spray oil and cook for 10 minutes or until the fish is cooked through, turning halfway through the cooking time.

To make the tartare sauce, combine the mayonnaise, gherkin, capers, mustard, lemon juice and dill or parsley.

Serve the fish with the chunky chips, mushy peas, tartare sauce and tomato ketchup.

CREAMY CHICKEN, BACON AND LEEK PIE

SERVES 6

This delicious pie comes together in less than 30 minutes and is all done in the air fryer. Depending on the size of your air fryer, this recipe will make either one big pie or two smaller pies.

⏲ Cooking time: 25 minutes

🍳 Preparation time: 5 minutes

♡ Calories: 340 kcals per serving

For the pie filling

4 chicken breasts (around 600g in weight), cut into bite-sized chunks

Non-stick spray oil

1 teaspoon garlic paste

1 teaspoon cornflour

6 smoked streaky bacon rashers, sliced

1 leek, sliced

3 tablespoons crème fraîche

1 teaspoon wholegrain mustard

50ml chicken stock

Salt and freshly ground black pepper

For the pie top

1 sheet of ready-rolled puff pastry (you may only need half a sheet to top the pie, depending on the size of your dish)

1 egg, beaten

COOK'S TIP

If you have enough meat left over from a roast chicken dinner, you can always use it to create this pie filling.

Preheat the air fryer to 180°C.

Place the chicken pieces in a bowl, season with salt and pepper and spray with a little non-stick spray oil.

Add the garlic paste and cornflour to the bowl and make sure all the chicken pieces are evenly coated.

Take a heatproof pie dish or foil tray that fits in your air fryer and spray generously with spray oil. (Depending on the size of your air fryer, or whether it has one or two drawers, you may need to make two smaller pies.)

Add the chicken to the dish, place in the air fryer and cook at 180°C for 7 minutes. Take the dish out and give everything a good stir to ensure it all cooks evenly. Now, add the sliced bacon and cook at 180°C for a further 5 minutes.

Next, add the sliced leek to the dish, mix well and cook at 180°C for a further 3 minutes, being careful not to burn the leeks.

Stir the crème fraîche, mustard and stock into the chicken pie filling.

Unroll the puff pastry sheet and cut it to the size of your dish or dishes. Brush the rim of the dish or dishes with the beaten egg, then lay the pastry over the pie filling. Brush the pastry top with the beaten egg and make a few holes in the pastry to allow steam to escape.

Reduce the temperature of the air fryer to 160°C. Place the pie in the air fryer and cook at 160°C for 10 minutes or until the pastry top has puffed up and is golden brown.

ROAST BEEF

SERVES
4

A joint of beef roasts perfectly in an air fryer, and it's just so easy. I've listed the timings in this recipe so that you can achieve the perfect well-done, medium or rare beef, depending on how you prefer yours cooked. Don't forget to save some slices for my Yorkshire Pudding Wraps with Roast Beef on page 111.

Cooking time: 30–50 minutes

Preparation time: 10 minutes

Calories: 367 kcals per serving

For the beef

1 medium beef roasting joint with fat (around 1kg in weight)

1 onion, roughly chopped

1 carrot, roughly chopped

1 tablespoon olive oil

1 teaspoon dried rosemary

Salt and freshly ground black pepper

Take the beef joint out of the fridge, remove all the packaging and string, then set aside for 30 minutes before cooking to allow the meat to come to room temperature.

Put the chopped onion and carrot in the bottom of the air fryer basket.

Rub the beef joint with the oil, sprinkle over the dried rosemary and season well with salt and pepper.

Place the beef joint in the air fryer, sitting it on top of the vegetables, and cook at 180°C, turning the meat halfway through the cooking time. The cooking time will depend on the weight of the beef joint and how well you like your meat cooked:

For rare, cook the beef at 180°C for 15 minutes for every 450g in weight.

For medium-rare, cook the beef at 180°C for 15 minutes for every 450g in weight, plus an extra 5 minutes at the end.

For medium, cook the beef at 180°C for 15 minutes for every 450g in weight, plus an extra 10 minutes at the end.

For medium-well, cook the beef at 180°C for 15 minutes for every 450g in weight, plus an extra 15 minutes at the end.

For well done, cook the beef at 180°C for 15 minutes for every 450g in weight, plus an extra 20 minutes at the end.

If you're unsure if the beef is cooked to your liking, use a digital probe thermometer to check the temperature of the meat. For rare, the beef should be 50°C. For medium, the beef should be 60°C. For well done, the beef should be 70°C.

Take the beef out of the air fryer, cover with a foil tent and allow to rest for 10 minutes before carving.

CHORIZO AND HALLOUMI KEBABS

SERVES
4

These kebabs are just so moreish. Any dish that combines halloumi with chorizo and, well, I'm there. I like to serve these with a crisp green salad to bring those summer vibes!

Cooking time: 13 minutes

Preparation time: 10 minutes

Calories: 647 kcals per serving

For the kebabs

200g chorizo ring

2 blocks halloumi

1 red onion, cut into small wedges

1 red pepper, cut into bite-sized chunks

1 yellow pepper, cut into bite-sized chunks

1 tablespoon runny honey

1 teaspoon smoked paprika

¼ teaspoon chilli flakes

Non-stick spray oil

If you're using wooden skewers, soak them in water for 30 minutes before cooking,

Slice the chorizo into 2cm thick rounds. Chop the halloumi into similar size chunks.

Thread the chorizo, halloumi and vegetables onto 8 small skewers.

Preheat the air fryer to 200°C.

Brush the skewers all over with the honey, then sprinkle over the paprika and chilli flakes.

Place the skewers in the air fryer. Spray with non-stick spray oil and cook at 200°C for 7 minutes. Turn the skewers over and cook for a further 6 minutes or until golden.

SWEET CHILLI STEAK STIR-FRY

This is so delicious, so quick and so easy. You can add whatever veggies you like to this stir-fry, or you can cheat and use a stir-fry veg mix!

Cooking time: 18 minutes

Preparation time: 10 minutes

Calories: 497 kcals per serving

For the stir-fry

1 fillet steak (or any other cut of steak, around 225g in weight)

100g Tenderstem broccoli

½ red pepper, thinly sliced

100g mushrooms, thinly sliced

½ carrot, thinly sliced

Non-stick spray oil

1 pack ready-cooked noodles (or 2 portions boiled noodles)

For the marinade

2 tablespoons soy sauce

2 tablespoons sweet chilli sauce

1 tablespoon tomato ketchup

¼ teaspoon chilli flakes

1 tablespoon sesame oil

1 teaspoon garlic paste

1 teaspoon ginger paste

To serve

2 spring onions, thinly sliced

1 red chilli, thinly sliced

Combine all the ingredients for the marinade in a bowl. Place the steak in separate bowl and pour over half of the marinade. Leave the steak to marinate for at least 30 minutes.

When ready to cook, preheat the air fryer to 200°C.

Place the steak in the air fryer and cook for 8 minutes, flipping over halfway through the cooking time. (This will give you a medium steak.) Loosely wrap the steak in foil and leave to rest while you make the stir-fry.

If you can, take the crisper plate out of the air fryer. If you can't, line the air fryer.

Reduce the temperature of the air fryer to 180°C. Place the vegetables in the air fryer, spray with non-stick spray oil and cook at 180°C for 6 minutes.

Add the noodles to the air fryer with the rest of the marinade, mix everything well and cook at 180°C for a further 4 minutes.

Slice the steak into thin strips. Divide the stir-fry between two bowls and top with the sliced steak. Scatter over the spring onions and red chilli before serving.

MEATBALL SUBS

SERVES 4

Who doesn't love a meatball sub? I know I definitely do. This meatball recipe is equally as delicious served over some spaghetti as it is in a sub. However you serve it, add plenty of cheese!

Cooking time: 17 minutes

Preparation time: 15 minutes

Calories: 537 kcals per serving

For the meatballs

500g minced beef (preferably 10% fat as it adds flavour and juiciness)

1 egg, beaten

1 onion, very finely diced or grated

2 tablespoons panko breadcrumbs

3 garlic cloves, minced

1 teaspoon dried oregano

1 teaspoon dried basil

1 teaspoon chilli flakes

400g tomato pasta sauce from a jar (or use my Marinara Sauce recipe on page 207)

Salt and freshly ground black pepper

To serve

4 sub bread rolls

50g mozzarella cheese, grated

Combine the minced beef, beaten egg, diced onion, panko breadcrumbs, garlic, dried oregano, dried basil and chilli flakes. Season with a good pinch each of salt and pepper. Roll the beef mixture into 12 equal-sized balls.

Preheat the air fryer to 180°C.

Place the meatballs in the air fryer, leaving space between each one, and cook at 180°C for 12 minutes or until cooked through, turning halfway through the cooking time.

Warm the tomato sauce in a bowl in the microwave until hot, then add to the cooked meatballs.

Slice open the sub rolls. Fill each sub with 3 meatballs, then scatter over the mozzarella. Return the filled subs to the air fryer and cook at 180°C for 5 minutes or until the cheese has melted and the subs have crisped up.

CHICKEN SKEWERS WITH SATAY PEANUT SAUCE

SERVES
4

These deliciously easy chicken skewers drizzled with satay peanut sauce will go down well with all the family, I guarantee it. These skewers are great served on top of jasmine rice with some steamed pak choi.

Cooking time: 12 minutes

Preparation time: 15 minutes

Calories: 478 kcals per serving

For the skewers and sauce

4 chicken breasts

3 tablespoons smooth peanut butter

2 tablespoons coconut milk

3 tablespoons dark soy sauce

1 tablespoon medium curry powder

1 tablespoon brown sugar

1 teaspoon garlic paste

1 teaspoon ginger paste

½ teaspoon chilli flakes

To serve

200g jasmine rice, cooked according to the packet instructions

2 pak choi, halved and steamed

Slice the chicken breasts into thin strips.

In a large bowl, combine 1 tablespoon of the peanut butter, 1 tablespoon of the coconut milk, 1 tablespoon of the soy sauce, 1 teaspoon each of the curry powder and brown sugar, and the garlic paste, ginger paste and chilli flakes. Stir well to make the marinade.

Add the chicken to the bowl with the marinade and stir well to make sure every piece is well coated. Leave the chicken to marinate in the fridge for at least 30 minutes. Meanwhile, soak some wooden skewers in cold water.

Take the chicken out of the fridge 15 minutes before cooking to allow the meat to come to room temperature. Thread the chicken onto the soaked wooden skewers.

When ready to cook, preheat the air fryer to 180°C.

Place the chicken skewers in the air fryer and cook at 180°C for 7 minutes. Turn the skewers over and cook for a further 5 minutes, or until the chicken is cooked through.

Meanwhile, make the satay peanut sauce. Combine the remaining peanut butter, coconut milk, soy sauce and brown sugar in a bowl and mix well. If the dipping sauce is too thick, add a splash of water and gently warm the sauce in the microwave for a minute or so to loosen.

Serve the chicken skewers on top of jasmine rice with some pak choi on the side. Drizzle over the satay peanut sauce before serving, leaving any extra in a bowl for people to help themselves to more.

ROAST CHICKEN

SERVES 4

Rotisserie-style chicken done at home in the air fryer! You can use the roasted chicken for so many dishes – from Sunday roasts, to pies, to curries and sandwiches. Nowadays, most air fryers are large enough to cook a whole chicken. Check your air fryer and as long as the chicken fits in and doesn't touch the top of the air fryer, you can do it!

🔔 Cooking time: 60 minutes

☕ Preparation time: 5 minutes

♡ Calories: 280 kcals per serving

For the chicken

1 medium whole chicken (around 1.6kg in weight)

1 tablespoon olive oil

2 teaspoons smoked paprika

2 teaspoons Cajun seasoning

Salt and freshly ground black pepper

To serve

Crispy Garlic Hasselback Potatoes (see page 154)

Roasted Vegetables (see page 148)

Preheat the air fryer to 180°C.

Drizzle the chicken with the olive oil and season with the smoked paprika, Cajun seasoning, salt and pepper. Rub the chicken all over on both sides to ensure it is fully coated.

Place the chicken breast side down in the air fryer, making sure it is not touching the top of the air fryer, and cook at 180°C for 30 minutes.

After 30 minutes, carefully flip the chicken over using heatproof tongs, add an extra drizzle of oil and cook at 180°C for a further 30 minutes.

Take the chicken out of the air fryer. If you have a digital probe thermometer, check the temperature of the thickest part of the chicken is at least 75°C. If you don't have a probe thermometer, make sure that the juices are running clear and the meat is not pink. A larger chicken might need longer in the air fryer, so check it after 1 hour and give it more time, if necessary.

Cover the chicken with foil and leave to rest before carving. Serve with hasselback potatoes and roasted vegetables.

COOK'S TIP

You can use different seasonings, if you prefer. For classic roast dinner flavours, use ½ teaspoon each of dried rosemary, thyme and sage.

KATSU CHICKEN BURGERS

A flavour sensation, these crispy chicken burgers are topped with katsu mayonnaise and served with a homemade slaw. You can also use plant-based 'chicken' burgers to make these vegetarian.

Cooking time: 20 minutes

Preparation time: 10 minutes

Calories: 570 kcals per serving

For the chicken

2 chicken breasts

2 tablespoons plain flour

1 egg, beaten

50g panko breadcrumbs

Salt and freshly ground black pepper

Non-stick spray oil

For the slaw

¼ red small cabbage, finely sliced

1 carrot, grated

2 spring onions, sliced

6 jalapeños and a splash of pickling juice from the jar

1 teaspoon rice wine vinegar

1 teaspoon soy sauce

1 teaspoon runny honey

For the katsu mayo

2 tablespoons 'light' mayonnaise

2 teaspoons medium curry powder

1 teaspoon runny honey

1 teaspoon soy sauce

To serve

2 brioche buns, sliced

First, make the katsu mayo. Combine the mayonnaise, curry powder, honey and soy sauce in a bowl. Stir well and set aside.

Next, make the slaw. Combine the red cabbage, carrot and spring onions in a bowl. Add a splash of pickling juice from the jar of jalapeños, the rice wine vinegar, soy sauce and honey. Mix well and set aside in the fridge while you prepare the burgers.

Preheat the air fryer to 180°C.

Prepare the chicken. Butterfly the chicken breasts, then season them with salt and pepper.

Organise your breading station by placing the flour in a shallow bowl and season with salt and pepper. In a second bowl, beat the egg. In a third bowl, combine the panko breadcrumbs with a little salt and pepper.

Coat the butterflied chicken first in the flour, then dip it into the beaten egg and finally into the panko breadcrumbs, making sure it is fully coated.

Place the breadcrumbed chicken in the air fryer and spray with non-stick spray oil. Cook at 180°C for 20 minutes or until golden and cooked through, turning halfway through the cooking time.

Add the brioche burger buns to the air fryer to toast for 1 minute before the end of the cooking time.

To assemble the burgers, place a good handful of the slaw on the bottom half of the brioche burger buns. Nestle the crispy chicken fillets on top of the slaw. Spread the tops of the buns with the katsu mayo and sit the bun on top of the chicken.

YORKSHIRE PUDDING WRAPS WITH ROAST BEEF

SERVES
1

Making Yorkshire puddings in the air fryer produces unbelievably good results – just make sure you don't open the drawer for at least 20 minutes to keep that rise. Used as wraps, you can fill them with whatever leftovers you have from the Sunday roast, but I love beef the best. They're just amazing.

Cooking time: 25 minutes

Preparation time: 10 minutes

Calories: 280 kcals per serving

For the Yorkshire pudding wrap

1 egg

70ml semi-skimmed milk

30g plain flour

15 sprays vegetable spray oil

Salt and freshly ground black pepper

To serve

1 tablespoon horseradish sauce

2 slices of roast beef (see page 98)

4 roast potatoes

Your favourite gravy

Place the egg, milk and flour in a bowl and whisk together until smooth. Season with a pinch each of salt and pepper. Set aside the batter to rest for at least 30 minutes or in the fridge overnight.

Preheat the air fryer to 180°C.

Use a foil tray or cake tin that will fit into your air fryer. Add the vegetable oil to the tray and place in the air fryer for 5 minutes to heat up.

Pour the batter into the tray. It should sizzle. Cook in the air fryer at 180°C for 20 minutes. Do not open the air fryer during this cooking time.

Take the Yorkshire pudding out of the air fryer. Turn it over and flatten it down. Spread the horseradish sauce over the flattened Yorkshire pudding, then fill with the sliced roast beef, roasties and gravy.

Roll up and wrap the ends in foil. Serve with a jug of extra gravy to pour over.

CHAPTER

4

FAKEAWAYS

SMASH BURGERS

SERVES
4

Smashing burger patties flat before cooking them in the air fryer ensures a delicious meaty crust. Customise your burger with any toppings that you like but do try my homemade burger sauce. It's absolutely amazing!

Cooking time: 8 minutes

Preparation time: 10 minutes

Calories: 413 kcals per serving

For the burgers

500g beef mince (5% fat)

8 cheese slices

For the burger sauce

2 tablespoons tomato ketchup

2 tablespoons 'light' mayonnaise

1 tablespoon mustard

2 pickled gherkins

To serve

4 brioche burger buns

Shredded iceberg lettuce

Your choice of toppings, such as sliced tomatoes, finely diced red onion and more finely diced pickled gherkins

COOK'S TIP

If you're making a large number of burgers to feed a gathering, wrap the burgers individually in foil to keep them warm – this also adds to the fast-food look!

Preheat the air fryer to 190°C.

Divide the minced beef into 8 equal-sized portions, then roll them into balls.

To make the thin burger patties, cover each ball of minced beef with a piece of parchment paper, then lightly bash them down to 1cm thick. (The patties will shrink as they cook, so make sure they are bashed out very thinly.)

Season both sides of each patty with salt and pepper.

Place the patties in the air fryer and cook at 190°C for 3 minutes, then flip over and cook for a further 3 minutes on the other side.

After 6 minutes, lay a cheese slice on top of each burger and add the sliced brioche buns to the air fryer. Cook everything for a further 2 minutes at 190°C.

Meanwhile, make the burger sauce. Combine the ketchup, mayo and mustard in a small bowl. Finely chop the gherkins and add those to the bowl and stir to mix well.

Next, assemble the burgers. Cover the bottom half of the buns with some of the burger sauce, then add a small handful of shredded iceberg lettuce.

Place a patty with cheese on top of the lettuce, then stack another patty with cheese on top of that.

Add your choice of toppings to the burger – I like thinly sliced tomatoes with finely diced red onion and gherkins.

Lastly, spread a little more burger sauce over the top half of the bun and sit it on top of the burger.

SPICY BEAN BURGERS WITH CHIPOTLE MAYO

I've always loved a spicy bean burger, and now my daughters do too. I make them with a combination of different beans plus lots of hidden veggies – perfect for those meat-free days. The spicy burgers are given even more of a kick here with the smoky chipotle mayo.

Cooking time: 16 minutes

Preparation time: 15 minutes

Calories: 498 kcals per serving

For the bean burgers

50g red lentils

1 x 400-g can kidney beans

1 x 400-g can mixed beans (or taco beans)

1 x 200-g can sweetcorn kernels

4 spring onions, chopped

1 red pepper, diced

1 chilli, diced

1 teaspoon garlic paste

50g golden breadcrumbs

2 teaspoons ground cumin

2 teaspoons smoked paprika

1 teaspoon cayenne pepper

4 cheese slices

For the chipotle mayo

4 tablespoons 'light' mayonnaise

1 teaspoon chipotle paste

To serve

4 brioche burger buns

1 little gem lettuce, leaves separated

1 large tomato, thinly sliced

Sweet Potato Fries (see page 203)

First, make the bean burgers. Cook the lentils following the instructions on the packet, then set aside.

Combine the beans in a large mixing bowl and mash them together, leaving a few chunkier bits.

Now, add the cooked lentils, sweetcorn, spring onions, red pepper, chilli, garlic, breadcrumbs, cumin, paprika, cayenne and a pinch each of salt and pepper. Give everything a really good mix.

Divide the spicy bean mixture into 4 equal-sized portions, then roll them into balls. Form each ball into a patty. If you have a burger press or a round mould this can help, but the don't need to be perfect!

Preheat the air fryer to 180°C.

Spray the patties with oil, place them in the air fryer and cook at 180°C for 7 minutes, then flip over and cook for a further 7 minutes on the other side until golden and crispy.

After 14 minutes, lay a cheese slice on top of each burger and add the sliced brioche buns to the air fryer. Cook everything for a further 2 minutes at 180°C.

Meanwhile, combine the mayo and chipotle paste in a small bowl and stir to mix well.

Next, assemble the burgers. Cover the bottom half of the buns with some of the chipotle mayo, then add a lettuce leaf and slices of tomato.

Place a bean burger with cheese on top of the salad.

Lastly, spread a little more chipotle mayo over the top half of the bun and sit it on top of the bean burger.

Serve with a side of sweet potato fries.

TANDOORI PANEER KEBABS

SERVES
2

These tandoori kebabs are made using the Indian cheese, paneer, which absorbs all the delicious flavours of the marinade. They make a healthier alternative to your usual takeaway. Quick, easy to make, full of flavour and vegetarian too.

Cooking time: 10 minutes

Preparation time: 10 minutes

Calories: 555 kcals per serving

For the kebabs

1 x 225-g block of paneer

½ red onion, cut into chunks

½ red pepper, cut into chunks

½ yellow pepper, cut into chunks

For the marinade

3 tablespoons natural yogurt

1 teaspoon garlic paste

1 teaspoon ginger paste

1 teaspoon garam masala

1 teaspoon chilli powder

1 teaspoon paprika

1 teaspoon ground coriander

1 teaspoon ground turmeric

Juice of ½ lemon

For the yogurt sauce

3 tablespoons natural yogurt

¼ cucumber, finely diced

1 teaspoon mint sauce

Juice of ½ lemon

To serve

2 naans or flatbreads

2 tablespoons mango chutney

Cut the paneer into 10 equal-sized chunks.

Make a marinade by mixing the yogurt in a bowl with the garlic paste, ginger paste, garam masala, chilli powder, paprika, coriander, turmeric and lemon juice.

Add the chopped paneer, red onion and red and yellow peppers to the bowl, stir to coat in the marinade. Leave to marinate in the fridge for 30 minutes.

When ready to cook, preheat the air fryer to 180°C.

Thread the marinated paneer and vegetables onto two long skewers (or four smaller skewers, depending on the size of your air fryer).

Place the skewers in the air fryer, spray with non-stick spray oil and cook at 180°C for 5 minutes. Turn the skewers and cook for a further 5 minutes.

Meanwhile, make the yogurt sauce. Combine the yogurt, cucumber, mint sauce and lemon juice in a small bowl.

Serve on naan or flatbreads with mango chutney and the yogurt sauce on the side.

LOADED DIRTY FRIES

SERVES
2

These dirty fries will satisfy your takeaway urge by bringing all of the cheesy goodness! You can enjoy these as a main dish or as a side as part of your Saturday-night feast.

Cooking time: 20 minutes

Preparation time: 10 minutes

Calories: 492 kcals per serving

For the fries

2 baking potatoes, unpeeled

Non-stick spray oil

1 teaspoon garlic paste

1 teaspoon smoked paprika

1 teaspoon Cajun seasoning

4 cheese slices

20ml milk

50g chorizo, finely diced

1 tablespoon pickled jalapeños, sliced

Salt and freshly ground black pepper

To serve

2 tablespoons sour cream

1 tablespoon salsa

2 spring onions, chopped

Slice the potatoes into thin-cut fries, leaving the skins on. Rinse under cold running water and then pat dry.

Microwave the potatoes on a plate for 4 minutes to kickstart the cooking.

Now, toss the potatoes in some spray oil in a large bowl. Add the garlic paste, smoked paprika, Cajun seasoning and a pinch each of salt and pepper, making sure all the fries are well coated.

Preheat the air fryer to 180°C.

Place the fries in the air fryer and cook for 15 minutes, shaking them a few times.

Once cooked, place the cheese slices in a heatproof bowl, add a splash of milk and microwave for 2 minutes or until it becomes a thick, cheesy sauce.

Pour the cheese sauce over the fries, then scatter over the chorizo and jalapeños. Cook in the air fryer at 180°C for a further 3 minutes or until the chorizo is warmed through.

Drizzle the loaded fries with the sour cream and salsa, then scatter over the chopped spring onions.

CHAR SUI PORK

SERVES 4

Cantonese-inspired, char sui pork with fluffy jasmine rice is such a tasty meal and something different to the usual takeaway. You do need to plan ahead when making this dish as the pork needs to marinate for a few hours before cooking.

△ Cooking time: 14 minutes

🍲 Preparation time: 10 minutes

♡ Calories: 521 kcals per serving

For the pork

4 pork shoulder steaks (around 650g in weight)

Non-stick spray oil

For the marinade

2 tablespoons dark soy sauce

2 tablespoons runny honey

1 tablespoon granulated white sugar

1 tablespoon hoisin sauce

1 tablespoon Chinese cooking wine (or Shaoxing rice wine, available in most large supermarkets, or dry sherry)

1 teaspoon garlic paste

½ teaspoon Chinese five spice powder

Few drops of red food colouring

To serve

200g jasmine rice, cooked according to the packet instructions

1 pak choi, steamed

First, make the marinade. Combine the soy sauce, honey, sugar, hoisin sauce, cooking or rice wine, garlic paste, Chinese five spice powder and food colouring in a bowl.

Set aside a few tablespoons of the marinade to use later to baste the pork while cooking.

Add the pork steaks to the rest of the marinade, making sure they are well coated.

Leave to marinate in the fridge for at least 3 hours, or preferably overnight.

When ready to cook, preheat the air fryer to 200°C.

Spray the air fryer with spray oil, place the pork steaks in the air fryer and cook for 6 minutes, then flip them over, brush with the reserved marinade for basting and cook for a further 6 minutes. Flip the pork steaks over once more and brush again with the marinade, then cook for a further 2 minutes.

Slice the pork thinly and serve over plain cooked jasmine rice with steamed pak choi.

CHICKEN PARMO WITH GARLIC DIP

This is a delicacy from the town of Middlesbrough, which is extremely popular across the North East of England. Crispy chicken is smothered in béchamel sauce and topped with cheese. My recipe is healthier than most takeaway versions and still tastes amazing. Although it is even more delicious with a side of chips!

Cooking time: 23 minutes

Preparation time: 10 minutes

Calories: 520 kcals per serving

For the chicken

2 chicken breasts

30g plain flour

1 egg, beaten

35g panko breadcrumbs

Non-stick spray oil

30g red Leicester cheese, grated

20g Cheddar cheese, grated

Salt and freshly ground black pepper

For the béchamel sauce

10g butter

10g plain flour

130ml semi-skimmed milk

Few gratings of nutmeg

For the garlic dip

1 tablespoon 'light' mayonnaise

1 tablespoon sour cream

½ teaspoon garlic paste

Preheat the air fryer to 180°C.

Prepare the chicken. Butterfly the chicken breasts to open them up, then cover in clingfilm and bash to flatten and make them thinner. Season well with salt and pepper.

Organise your breading station by placing the flour in a shallow bowl and season with salt and pepper. In a second bowl, beat the egg. In a third bowl, combine the panko breadcrumbs with a little salt and pepper.

Coat the butterflied chicken first in the flour, then dip it into the beaten egg and finally into the panko breadcrumbs, making sure it is fully coated.

Place the breadcrumbed chicken in the air fryer and spray with a generous amount of non-stick spray oil. Cook at 180°C for 18 minutes or until golden and cooked through, turning halfway through the cooking time.

Meanwhile, make the béchamel sauce. In a small pan, melt the butter over a medium heat, then whisk in the flour to form a paste. Gradually add in the milk, keep whisking adding a little more milk as you go. Grate in a little nutmeg and season with salt and pepper, cook until thickened.

Once the chicken is cooked, pour over the béchamel sauce and top with the grated cheeses. Cook in the air fryer at 180°C for 5 minutes.

Meanwhile, make the garlic dip. Combine the mayo, sour cream and garlic paste in a bowl.

Serve the chicken parmo with the garlic dip.

PERI-PERI GARLIC BREAD BURGER

SERVES 2

This peri-peri burger combines all of the flavours we know and love from everyone's favourite Portuguese chicken restaurant. And it takes no time at all to make your own version at home in the air fryer.

Cooking time: 10 minutes

Preparation time: 10 minutes

Calories: 625 kcals per serving

For the chicken

2 boneless, skinless chicken breasts

2 tablespoons of your favourite peri-peri marinade

For the garlic butter

1 tablespoon butter

½ teaspoon garlic paste

Small pinch of chopped parsley (either fresh or dried)

To serve

2 ciabatta rolls, sliced

80g 'light' halloumi

2 tablespoons chilli jam (see page 208 for homemade)

4 baby gem lettuce leaves

2 tablespoons peri-peri mayonnaise

Butterfly both the chicken breasts to open them up. Coat them in the peri-peri marinade and set aside to marinate for at least 10 minutes.

Make the garlic butter by mashing the butter in a bowl with ½ teaspoon garlic paste and a pinch of parsley. If the butter is too hard, microwave it for only a few seconds to soften it.

Spread the sliced ciabatta rolls with the garlic butter.

Coat the halloumi in 1 tablespoon of the chilli jam.

Place the marinated chicken in the air fryer. Spray with some spray oil and cook at 180°C for 10 minutes.

With 5 minutes of the cooking time left, add the halloumi to the air fryer and flip the chicken over. With 3 minutes of the cooking time left, add the garlic ciabatta to the air fryer to toast.

Assemble the burgers with the lettuce, chicken, halloumi, peri-peri mayo and remaining chilli jam.

CRISPY HONEY-GARLIC CHICKEN TENDERS

SERVES
2

These air-fried chicken tenders are much healthier than any deep-fried chicken from a takeaway bucket, and I think they taste even better. The honey-garlic glaze makes them totally addictive!

Cooking time: 14 minutes

Preparation time: 10 minutes

Calories: 404 kcals per serving

For the chicken

2 boneless, skinless chicken breasts

2 tablespoons plain flour

2 teaspoons smoked paprika

2 teaspoons garlic granules

40g cornflakes, crushed

1 egg

Salt and freshly ground black pepper

Non-stick spray oil

For the honey-garlic glaze

30g runny honey (for an extra kick, use hot honey infused with chilli)

30g sweet chilli sauce

15g dark soy sauce

1 teaspoon garlic paste

To serve

1 red chilli, sliced

2 spring onions, sliced

Preheat the air fryer to 180°C.

Slice the chicken breasts into long strips. Each breast should make 4 or 5 strips.

In a bowl, mix the flour with 1 teaspoon of the smoked paprika, 1 teaspoon of the garlic granules and a pinch each of salt and pepper.

In another bowl mix the crushed cornflakes with the remaining 1 teaspoon of smoked paprika, 1 teaspoon of garlic granules and a pinch each of salt and pepper.

Crack the egg into a third bowl and whisk it.

Dip each chicken strip first into the flour to coat, then into the beaten egg, and finally into the crushed cornflake mixture.

Place the coated chicken strips in the air fryer. Spray with non-stick spray oil and cook at 180°C for 14 minutes, turning the chicken halfway through the cooking time.

Meanwhile, make the honey-garlic glaze. Combine the honey, sweet chilli sauce, soy sauce and garlic paste in a small pan. Simmer the sauce over a low heat for a few minutes or until slightly thickened.

Once cooked, drizzle the honey-garlic glaze over the crispy chicken tenders, then scatter over some sliced red chillies and spring onions.

GREEK-STYLE CHICKEN GYROS

This classic Greek dish has such delicious fresh flavours, all brought together by homemade tzatziki. It really brings those delightful holiday vibes back home. Swap the chicken for halloumi if you want to make this recipe veggie-friendly.

Cooking time: 40 minutes

Preparation time: 10 minutes

Calories: 557 kcals per serving

For the chicken

450g boneless, skinless chicken thighs

For the marinade

3 tablespoons natural Greek yogurt

Juice of ½ lemon

2 tablespoons red wine vinegar

2 teaspoons garlic paste

1 teaspoon ground cumin

1 teaspoon smoked paprika

1 teaspoon dried oregano

For the tzatziki

4 tablespoons natural Greek yogurt

¼ cucumber, seeds scooped out and finely chopped

Juice of ½ lemon

½ teaspoon garlic paste

1 tablespoon chopped fresh mint

To serve

4 flatbreads (see page 205 for homemade)

2 handfuls of cherry tomatoes, quartered

¼ cucumber, thinly sliced

1 red onion, thinly sliced

Chunky Chips (see page 202, optional)

First, make the marinade. Combine the yogurt, lemon juice, vinegar, garlic paste, cumin, paprika, oregano and a pinch each of salt and pepper in a bowl.

Add the chicken to the marinade, making sure it is well coated. Leave to marinate in the fridge for at least 1 hour, or preferably overnight.

When ready to cook, preheat the air fryer to 180°C.

Thread the marinated chicken thighs onto two long skewers (or four smaller skewers, depending on the size of your air fryer).

Place the chicken skewers in the air fryer. Spray with non-stick spray oil and cook at 180°C for 20 minutes, then turn the skewers over, spray with more oil and cook for a further 20 minutes or until the chicken is cooked through. (If you have a digital probe thermometer, the thickest part of the chicken should be at least 165°C.)

In the last 20 minutes of cooking time for the chicken, cook the chips (see page 202). You can either cook them at 180°C in a separate drawer from the chicken or scatter them around the skewers if your air fryer has one drawer.

Meanwhile, make the tzatziki by combining all the ingredients in a small bowl with a small pinch of salt.

Once cooked, carve the chicken into chunky slices.

Assemble the gyros by layering the flatbreads with the chunks of chicken, tomato wedges, cucumber and red onion slices. You can include some chunky chips, if you like. Dot with dollops of the tzatziki, then roll up the flatbreads to make them into wraps.

BEEF FRIED RICE

SERVES 2

I love a good stir-fried rice dish, but perhaps they're something that you didn't realise you could make in an air fryer. The combination of juicy beef, crispy veggies and fluffy rice make the perfect fakeaway. Feel free to add some chilli flakes or hot sauce for extra spice.

Cooking time: 12 minutes

Preparation time: 15 minutes

Calories: 591 kcals per serving

For the beef

250g beef mince (5% fat)

2 tablespoons dark soy sauce

1 tablespoon sesame oil

1 tablespoon rice wine vinegar

1 tablespoon runny honey

1 teaspoon garlic paste

½ teaspoon ginger paste

½ teaspoon MSG (optional, but it really enhances the flavours)

Salt and freshly ground black pepper

Non-stick spray oil

For the rice

140g jasmine rice, cooked and still warm

100g broccoli, cooked and chopped into small pieces

50g frozen peas

½ red pepper, finely diced

2 spring onions, finely sliced

2 eggs, beaten

To serve

Your favourite hot sauce, such as sriracha

Preheat the air fryer to 180°C.

In a bowl, combine the minced beef with 1 tablespoon of the dark soy sauce, the sesame oil, rice wine vinegar, runny honey, garlic paste, ginger paste, MSG (if using) and a pinch each of salt and pepper.

Line the air fryer. Spray with non-stick spray oil and place the minced beef in the air fryer, scattering it over the drawer. Cook at 180°C for 6 minutes, stirring halfway through to break up any clumps of meat.

Once the beef is cooked, add the warm cooked rice and vegetables to the air fryer. Give everything a good stir to make sure it's all well mixed.

Pour in the beaten eggs, spray with non-stick spray oil and cook everything together at 180°C for 3 minutes.

After 3 minutes, give everything another good stir, breaking the eggs up into the rice. Add the remaining soy sauce and cook for a further 3 minutes.

Divide the beef fried rice between individual bowls and serve with your favourite hot sauce alongside.

CHICKEN TIKKA KEBABS

You can't beat a chicken tikka kebab. Serve these however you like, they are so delicious in a pita bread with lots of salad, raita and chilli sauce.

Cooking time: 15 minutes

Preparation time: 10 minutes

Calories: 240 kcals per serving

For the kebabs

2 chicken breasts

2 tablespoons tikka curry paste

4 tablespoons natural yogurt

1 small red onion, cut into wedges

½ red pepper, cut into bite-sized chunks

½ yellow pepper, cut into bite-sized chunks

Non-stick spray oil

To serve

2 pita breads

Salad

Raita

Chilli sauce

Slice the chicken breasts into thin strips.

In a large bowl, combine the tikka curry paste with the yogurt. Add the chicken strips to the bowl and stir well to fully coat the chicken in the spicy yogurt. Marinate in the fridge for at least 1 hour or preferably overnight.

When ready to cook, thread the marinated chicken strips onto four skewers along with the red onion wedges and red and yellow pepper chunks.

Preheat air fryer to 180°C.

Place the chicken tikka skewers in the air fryer and spray with non-stick spray oil. Cook in the air fryer at 180°C for 15 minutes, or until the chicken is cooked through, turning them halfway through the cooking time.

Serve the kebabs in the pita breads, filled with salad and drizzled with raita and chilli sauce.

CHEESEBURGER TACOS

These cheeseburger tacos are absolutely delicious and so easy to put together. If cooking for more than one person you'll just need to do them in batches.

- Cooking time: 9 minutes
- Preparation time: 5 minutes
- Calories: 450 kcals per serving

For the cheeseburger tacos

100g beef mince (5% fat)

2 mini tortillas

2 cheese slices

Salt and freshly ground black pepper

To serve

2 tablespoons burger sauce

Chopped lettuce, sliced tomatoes, sliced red onion and sliced pickled gherkins or your favourite toppings

Divide the minced beef into 2 equal-sized portions. Spread one half over each of the mini tortillas. Season well with salt and pepper.

Cook the tortillas in the air fryer at 180°C for 8 minutes or until the minced beef is cooked through.

Top the tortillas with the cheese slices and return to the air fryer and cook for 1 minute to melt the cheese.

Top the cheeseburger with the burger sauce and all of your favourite toppings.

SALT AND CHILLI CHICKEN SPICE BAGS

SERVES 2

Spice bags are super popular in Ireland and they have since gone viral online. And I can see why. Crispy salt and chilli chicken and chips are served in a paper bag at many Irish-Chinese takeaways. Totally delicious with curry sauce!

⏱ Cooking time: 27 minutes

🍲 Preparation time: 15 minutes

♡ Calories: 606 kcals per serving

For the chicken and chips

2 boneless, skinless chicken breasts, thinly sliced

2 tablespoons plain flour

1 egg

50g panko breadcrumbs

300g steak-cut frozen chips

Non-stick spray oil

½ red pepper

½ green pepper

1 onion

2 red chillies, sliced

For the spice mix

1 teaspoon Chinese five spice powder

1 teaspoon granulated white sugar

1 teaspoon chilli flakes

½ teaspoon salt

½ teaspoon freshly ground black pepper

½ teaspoon MSG (optional, but it really enhances the flavours)

To serve

Your favourite curry sauce

Preheat the air fryer to 180°C.

Slice the chicken breasts into long strips. Each breast should make 4 or 5 strips.

Place the flour in a bowl. In another bowl, whisk the egg. Place the panko breadcrumbs in a third bowl.

Start by dipping the sliced chicken in the flour, then the egg, then coating in the panko breadcrumbs.

Make your spice mix by combining the Chinese five spice powder, sugar, chilli flakes, salt, pepper and MSG (if using).

Place the frozen chips in the air fryer. Cook for 10 minutes or until starting to look cooked, shaking halfway through.

Remove the partially cooked chips, then add the chicken to the air fryer, spray with plenty of non-stick spray oil and cook at 180°C for 12 minutes or until golden on both sides, turning halfway through.

Next, return the partially cooked chips to the air fryer with the chicken, along with the veg, shake the spices over and give everything a good mix and spray with oil, cook everything together for a further 5 minutes or until everything is golden and cooked through.

For the proper takeaway experience, serve portions of the chicken and chips in a paper bag – of course, you can use plates – with your favourite curry sauce.

COOK'S TIP

For a very simple curry sauce, I mix curry paste with water to make the thin paste and then microwave it following the instructions on the packet.

SWEET AND SOUR CHICKEN

SERVES
2

Sweet and sour chicken is such a popular takeaway dish, it never falls out of favour. It's usually deep-fried, but this air-fryer version keeps all of the taste without the oil. Enjoy this sweet and sour chicken with some of the other Chinese fakeaway dishes in this chapter for a mighty feast!

Cooking time: 13 minutes

Preparation time: 5 minutes

Calories: 389 kcals per serving

For the chicken

2 chicken breasts, chopped into bite-sized chunks

2 tablespoons cornflour

Non-stick spray oil

½ red pepper, chopped into bite-sized chunks

½ green pepper, chopped into bite-sized chunks

½ onion, chopped into bite-sized chunks

1 x 200-g can pineapple chunks

Salt and freshly ground black pepper

For the sauce

2 tablespoons ketchup

2 tablespoons dark soy sauce

2 tablespoons rice wine vinegar

2 tablespoons granulated sugar

1 teaspoon garlic paste

2 tablespoons pineapple juice from the can

To serve

200g jasmine rice, cooked according to the packet instructions

Preheat the air fryer to 180°C.

In a bowl, season the chicken with salt and pepper, then combine the chunks of chicken with the cornflour, until evenly coated, shake off any excess.

Spray the air fryer with a little non-stick spray oil, then add the chunks of chicken, spray the chicken generously with some oil and cook at 180°C for 8–10 minutes or until lightly golden all over, turning halfway to ensure even cooking.

After 10 minutes, add the chopped peppers and onions and cook for a further 3 minutes.

Meanwhile in a microwavable bowl, mix together the ketchup, soy sauce, rice wine vinegar, sugar and garlic paste, gently microwave for 1 minute bursts, stirring in-between until thickened (or thicken on the hob).

In a bowl, combine the chicken, peppers and onions with the pineapple chunks and mix through the warmed sweet and sour sauce.

Serve the sweet and sour chicken on a bed of cooked jasmine rice.

CRISPY CHILLI BEEF

SERVES 2

This is one of my favourite meals for a night in with the girls. The juicy but crispy beef with just a hint of spice is divine!

Cooking time: 13 minutes

Preparation time: 10 minutes

Calories: 481 kcals per serving

For the beef

2 sirloin steaks (around 350g in weight), sliced into thin strips

1 small egg, beaten

2 tablespoons cornflour

Non-stick spray oil

1 small onion, sliced into thin strips

½ red bell pepper, sliced into thin strips

1 red chilli, sliced

1 teaspoon garlic paste

1 teaspoon ginger paste

2 tablespoons rice wine vinegar

2 tablespoons dark soy sauce

2 tablespoons sweet chilli sauce

2 tablespoons tomato ketchup

1 tablespoon tomato purée

2 teaspoons granulated white sugar

Salt and freshly ground black pepper

To serve

1 teaspoon sesame seeds

In a bowl, combine the thinly sliced beef with the egg. Add the cornflour with a pinch each of salt and pepper and mix well to coat the beef.

Preheat air fryer to 180°C.

Spray the air fryer with non-stick spray oil, add the beef, leaving room between each slice. Spray all over with more oil and then cook at 180°C for 10 minutes or until crispy.

Remove the beef once crispy, add the onion, red pepper and chilli, spray with oil and cook for 3 minutes or until softened.

Make the sauce by combining the garlic paste, ginger paste, rice wine vinegar, dark soy sauce, sweet chilli sauce, tomato ketchup, tomato purée and sugar in a microwaveable bowl. Microwave in 1-minute bursts, stirring in between, until thickened (or just thicken up on the hob).

Divide the crispy beef between bowls with the veg and sauce. Sprinkle over the sesame seeds before serving.

DONER KEBABS WITH GARLIC SAUCE

SERVES 4

Enjoy a guilt-free kebab in the comfort of your own home with this delicious recipe. Perfect with lamb mince as an alternative too!

Cooking time: 45 minutes

Preparation time: 15 minutes

Calories: 389 kcals per serving

For the kebabs

500g beef mince (12% fat)

1 tablespoon harissa paste

1 teaspoon dried oregano

1 teaspoon ground cumin

1 teaspoon onion powder

2 teaspoons garlic paste

½ teaspoon chilli flakes

1 teaspoon smoked paprika

Salt and freshly ground black pepper

For the garlic sauce

1 garlic bulb

Non-stick spray oil

2 tablespoons 'light' mayonnaise

2 tablespoons natural yogurt

Juice of ½ lemon

½ teaspoon dried oregano

To serve

4 pita breads or flatbreads

Salad such as sliced red onion, sliced cucumber, halved cherry tomatoes and chopped or shredded lettuce

Preheat the air fryer to 180°C.

In a bowl, combine the minced beef with a pinch each of salt and pepper, add the harissa paste, oregano, cumin, onion powder, garlic paste, chilli flakes and paprika.

Shape the meat into a large tube shape, roll in foil.

Cut the top off the garlic bulb, spray with a little oil and wrap in foil.

Preheat the air fryer to 180°C.

Place the kebab and garlic, both in foil, in the air fryer and cook at 180°C for 35 minutes.

Take out the kebab and leave to rest for 10 minutes while you prepare the garlic sauce.

The garlic cloves should squeeze out easily from their skins. If they don't, return them to the air fryer for a further 5–10 minutes.

Squeeze the roasted garlic into a bowl, mash up, then mix with the mayo, yogurt, lemon juice and oregano.

Warm up the pita breads or flatbreads. Meanwhile, thinly slice the kebab meat.

Spread the warmed breads with the garlic sauce. Layer on the doner kebab meat, red onion, cucumber, tomatoes and lettuce. Serve any remaining garlic sauce alongside.

CAJUN PRAWN TACOS

SERVES
4

I absolutely love the spicy, smoky flavours in Cajun seasoning, especially with the natural sweetness of corn-on-the-cobs. So delicious! You can swap out the prawns for any sustainable white fish or it's also really yummy with chicken.

Cooking time: 20 minutes

Preparation time: 5 minutes

Calories: 486 kcals per serving

For the prawns

500g frozen king prawns, fully defrosted

Non-stick spray oil

3 teaspoons Cajun seasoning

1 lime

2 corn-on-the-cob

For the salsa

1 avocado, diced

150g cherry tomatoes, diced

½ red onion, diced

1 tablespoon chopped coriander or parsley

To serve

8 mini taco tortillas

4 tablespoons sriracha mayo (or mix plain mayo with your favourite hot sauce)

In a bowl, combine the prawns with a few sprays of oil, the Cajun seasoning and the juice of half the lime (save the other half to serve). Leave to marinate in the fridge for at least 30 minutes.

Preheat the air fryer to 180°C.

Add the corn cobs and spray with oil, cook for 12 minutes or until cooked through. Once cooked, remove and set aside.

Spray the air fryer with oil, add the prawns to the air fryer in a single layer and cook for 6 minutes or until cooked through.

Make the salsa by mixing the cubed avocado with the tomatoes, red onion, a squeeze of the lime and fresh coriander (or use parsley).

Slice the corn off of the cobs, leaving it in large chunks.

Warm the tacos in the microwave for 30 seconds or in the air fryer at 180°C for 2 minutes.

Serve the prawns on the tacos, with the salsa and corn, garnish with the lime. Drizzle with some sriracha mayo and enjoy!

EASY STUFFED CRUST PIZZA

SERVES
1

Making homemade pizzas is an easy and creative way to rustle up a meal for friends, as each pizza can be personalised with each guest's choice of favourite toppings. But because nobody likes a soggy pizza base, precook the base for a few minutes before adding the sauce and toppings.

Cooking time: 9 minutes

Preparation time: 15 minutes

Calories: 615 kcals per serving

For the pizza base

80g self-raising flour, plus extra to dust

85g natural yogurt

¼ teaspoon garlic granules

¼ teaspoon dried oregano

Non-stick spray oil

For the stuffed crust and topping

80g firm mozzarella for pizza (usually sold in blocks)

Pizza toppings of your choice, such as sliced pepperoni and chillies, diced ham and pineapple, anchovies and olives

For the pizza sauce

1 tablespoon tomato purée

1 teaspoon garlic paste

½ teaspoon dried oregano

Combine the flour, yogurt, garlic granules and oregano in a mixing bowl until a soft dough forms.

Dust a clean work surface with flour and roll out the dough into a thin pizza round. Make it a little larger than your air-fryer basket as once the edges of the base are folded inwards to make the stuffed crust it will be a bit smaller. If the base sticks to the work surface or rolling pin, just add a little bit more flour.

First, spray an air-fryer liner generously with non-stick spray oil and then transfer the rolled-out pizza dough onto it.

Chop up half of the firm mozzarella into small matchsticks. Arrange a circle of these mozzarella matchsticks all the way around the pizza base, just inside the edge. Fold the dough over the mozzarella matchsticks to make the stuffed crust, pressing down to ensure they're all covered. Spray the dough with more spray oil and brush it all over.

Preheat the air fryer to 180°C.

Lift the liner to transfer the pizza to the air fryer and cook at 180°C for 4 minutes. This starts to cook the pizza dough before the toppings are added to ensure it's crisp rather than soggy.

Meanwhile, make the pizza sauce by mixing the tomato purée with the garlic paste and oregano. Add a splash of water to bring it to the right consistency and stir.

After 4 minutes, spread the pizza with the pizza sauce, grate on the other half of the mozzarella and add your chosen toppings. Cook at 180°C for a further 5 minutes or until the cheese is bubbling and the pizza base is golden.

CHAPTER

5

SNACKS & SIDES

MEXICAN-STYLE CORN RIBS

Corn ribs are such a fun way to eat sweetcorn. I love the way the corn cobs curl up slightly while cooking to create that 'rib' shape, which makes it easy to bite off all the kernels. The perfect starter or side dish, you can easily double this recipe to feed a crowd. If so, you may need to cook them in batches.

Cooking time: 17 minutes

Preparation time: 10 minutes

Calories: 120 kcals per serving

For the corn ribs

2 corn-on-the-cob

1 tablespoon melted butter

¼ teaspoon smoked paprika

¼ teaspoon ground cumin

¼ teaspoon garlic paste

Salt and freshly ground black pepper

For the garlic dip

1 tablespoon 'light' mayonnaise

1 tablespoon sour cream

½ teaspoon garlic paste

To serve

1 lime, cut into wedges

20g Parmesan cheese, grated

¼ teaspoon chilli flakes

Handful of chopped fresh parsley

Put the corn cobs on a plate and microwave for 3 minutes to soften slightly. Once cool, very carefully slice the corn cobs in half all the way down the centre and then slice each half in half again to make 4 'ribs' from each corn cob.

In a bowl, mix together the melted butter with the smoked paprika, ground cumin and garlic paste with a pinch each of salt and pepper.

Brush the corn ribs with the spiced butter mixture.

Preheat the air fryer to 180°C.

Place the corn ribs in the air fryer in a single layer and cook at 180°C for 14 minutes or until cooked.

Meanwhile, make the garlic dip. Mix together the mayo, sour cream and garlic paste.

Remove the corn ribs from the air fryer and sprinkle with a squeeze of lime juice, then scatter over the Parmesan cheese, chilli flakes and parsley. Serve with the garlic dip and lime wedges for squeezing over.

ROASTED VEGETABLES

SERVES
4

Vibrant seasonal veggies, lightly roasted to perfection in the air fryer, are the perfect side to serve with so many different dishes. Delicious! Shown on page 106.

Cooking time: 12 minutes

Preparation time: 5 minutes

Calories: 93 kcals per serving

For the veggies

1 courgette, sliced

200g cherry tomatoes, kept whole

1 red onion, cut into bite-sized chunks

1 red pepper, cut into bite-sized chunks

1 yellow pepper, cut into bite-sized chunks

120g Tenderstem broccoli

1 tablespoon olive oil

1 teaspoon garlic paste

1 teaspoon dried oregano

Salt and freshly ground black pepper

Preheat the air fryer to 180°C.

Place the vegetables in a bowl, drizzle over the oil, then add the garlic paste and oregano. Season with a pinch each of salt and pepper.

Line the air fryer. Place the vegetables in the air fryer and cook at 180°C for 12 minutes or until cooked through, shaking halfway through the cooking time.

PANCETTA SPROUTS

Brussels sprouts are not just for Christmas! But forget those soggy sprouts of Christmas dinners past, cooking them in an air fryer gives them a crispier texture and more caramelised taste. This is my cheesy twist on a classic side dish.

Cooking time: 23 minutes

Preparation time: 10 minutes

Calories: 121 kcals per serving

For the sprouts

500g Brussels sprouts, peeled, trimmed and halved

Non-stick spray oil

65g pancetta or bacon lardons

30g Parmesan cheese, grated

Freshly ground black pepper

Place the Brussels sprouts in a microwave-safe dish with 100ml cold water. Cook in the microwave for 3 minutes to slightly soften.

Pat dry the sprouts, then place them in the air fryer basket. Spray with spray oil, then sprinkle over a little black pepper.

Cook in the air fryer at 180°C for 10 minutes. After 10 minutes, shake the sprouts and add the pancetta. Mix well and cook for a further 10 minutes, or until the sprouts are cooked through and caramelised.

Scatter the grated Parmesan cheese over the sprouts before serving.

ASPARAGUS WITH TOMATO AND PARMESAN

I love exploring new flavours and textures to keep veggies exciting, both for me and my daughters. This unique combination of asparagus spears with ripe cherry tomatoes and salty Parmesan is really, really tasty.

Cooking time: 10 minutes

Preparation time: 5 minutes

Calories: 119 kcals per serving

For the asparagus

400g asparagus spears

300g cherry tomatoes, halved

1 teaspoon olive oil

Juice of 1 lemon

40g Parmesan cheese, grated

Salt and freshly ground black pepper

To serve

Handful of fresh basil leaves

1 tablespoon balsamic glaze

Preheat the air fryer to 180°C.

Snap off the very bottom ends of the asparagus spears to remove the woody bits.

Place the asparagus spears and cherry tomatoes in a bowl, drizzle over the oil to coat. Add a squeeze of lemon juice and season with a pinch each of salt and pepper.

First, place the asparagus spears only in the air fryer and cook at 180°C for 5 minutes.

Next, add the tomatoes on top of the asparagus, scatter over the grated Parmesan cheese and cook at 180°C for a further 5 minutes.

Once cooked, arrange the asparagus spears and cherry tomatoes on a serving plate, scatter over the fresh basil, add another squeeze of lemon juice and drizzle over the balsamic glaze.

BANG BANG CAULIFLOWER

SERVES 4

Bite-sized cauliflower florets are battered, air-fried, then dunked in hot chilli bang bang sauce to make an utterly addictive snack.

🔔 Cooking time: 15 minutes

🍽 Preparation time: 15 minutes

♡ Calories: 299 kcals per serving

For the cauliflower

1 cauliflower

200ml buttermilk

80g plain flour

2 teaspoons cornflour

1 teaspoon onion powder

1 teaspoon garlic paste

80g panko breadcrumbs

Salt and freshly ground black pepper

Non-stick spray oil

For the bang bang sauce

3 tablespoons 'light' mayonnaise

3 tablespoons sweet chilli sauce

1 tablespoon sriracha hot chilli sauce

To serve

1 tablespoon sesame seeds

Sliced red chillies (optional)

Sliced spring onions (optional)

Preheat the air fryer to 190°C.

Remove the leaves from the cauliflower and cut the head into small florets.

Combine the buttermilk with the plain flour, cornflour, onion powder and garlic paste in a bowl to make a batter. Season with a pinch each of salt and pepper.

Place the panko breadcrumbs in a separate bowl and season with salt and pepper.

First, dip the cauliflower florets into the batter, lift them out and allow any excess batter to fall away. Next, roll the battered florets in the panko breadcrumbs to coat.

Place the coated cauliflower florets in the air fryer in a single layer. Spray with non-stick spray oil and cook at 190°C for 15 minutes or until crispy and golden.

Meanwhile, make the bang bang sauce. Mix together all the ingredients for the sauce in a bowl.

Once cooked, dip each cauliflower floret into the bang bang sauce and sprinkle over the sesame seeds. Scatter over some finely sliced red chillies and spring onions before serving, if you like.

CRISPY GARLIC HASSELBACK POTATOES

SERVES 4

There's something about a crispy potato that never fails to please. These hasselback potatoes are packed with flavour and will have you going back for more. Shown on page 106.

⏱ Cooking time: 20 minutes

⏲ Preparation time: 10 minutes

♡ Calories: 167 kcals per serving

For the potatoes

600g baby potatoes

1 tablespoon olive oil

2 teaspoons garlic paste

½ teaspoon smoked paprika

½ teaspoon dried oregano

30g Parmesan cheese, grated

Preheat the air fryer to 180°C.

First, prepare the potatoes. Take a potato and place a chopstick along both long sides. Using a sharp knife, carefully slice across the potato all the way down to the chopsticks – the chopsticks act as a buffer and will prevent you from slicing all the way through the potato. Make lots of cuts in the potato at 1–2mm intervals.

In a small bowl, mix the oil with the garlic paste, paprika and oregano.

Brush the potatoes all over with the oil mixture.

Place the potatoes in the air fryer and cook at 180°C for 10 minutes. Turn over the potatoes, scatter the grated Parmesan cheese all over and cook at 180°C for a further 10 minutes or until crispy and golden.

COOK'S TIP

Slice the hasselback potatoes as thinly as possible, but do not cut them all the way through – they must remain connected at the base. If you're unsure, there are lots on videos online showing how to prepare the potatoes.

CRISPY ONION RINGS

SERVES 2

I absolutely love onion rings. These are a much healthier version than deep-fried ones, but they're oh-so tasty! These onion rings are the perfect side dish to accompany the Smash Burgers (page 114) or Spicy Bean Burgers (page 116).

Cooking time: 10 minutes

Preparation time: 15 minutes

Calories: 132 kcals per serving

For the onion rings

2 large white onions, peeled

2 tablespoons plain flour

1 teaspoon paprika

1 egg, beaten

25g panko breadcrumbs

Salt and freshly ground black pepper

Non-stick spray oil

Your favourite sauce, to serve

Preheat the air fryer to 200°C.

Slice the onions into rounds and then separate each round into individual rings.

Organise your breading station by placing the flour in a shallow bowl and season with ½ teaspoon of the paprika and a pinch each of salt and pepper. In a second bowl, beat the egg. In a third bowl, combine the panko breadcrumbs with the remaining paprika and another pinch each of salt and pepper.

Working in batches, drop the onion rings first into the flour, making sure they are fully coated. Next, dip the floured onion rings in the beaten egg and then lift them to allow any excess to drip off. Lastly, place the onion rings into the panko breadcrumbs, making sure they are covered in the breadcrumbs on both sides.

Place the onion rings in the air fryer basket in a single layer to allow the hot air to circulate around them. Spray the onion rings very generously with spray oil. Cook at 200°C for 10 minutes or until the onion rings are crispy and golden, flipping them halfway through the cooking time.

Serve straight away while hot, with your favourite sauce.

CHEESY STUFFED MUSHROOMS

SERVES
4

Stuffed mushrooms are still a dinner-party classic. Why? Because they're the ultimate crowd pleaser. I use a three-cheese filling to stuff the caps of giant Portobello mushrooms to make a hearty snack.

Cooking time: 7 minutes

Preparation time: 10 minutes

Calories: 111 kcals per serving

For the mushrooms

4 Portobello or other large mushrooms

60g 'light' cream cheese

30g mozzarella, grated

20g Parmesan cheese, grated

3 spring onions, sliced

30g golden breadcrumbs

Salt and freshly ground black pepper

Handful of finely chopped chives, to serve

Preheat the air fryer to 180°C.

First, prepare the mushrooms. Remove the stems and gently rub the caps with a paper towel to remove any dirt. With the mushrooms stem side up, scoop out the dark gills using a teaspoon to make a 'bowl'. Pat the mushrooms dry.

Mix together the cream cheese, mozzarella and Parmesan cheese in a bowl. Stir in the sliced spring onions and season with a pinch each of salt and pepper. Place the breadcrumbs in a separate bowl.

Spoon the cheesy mixture into the 'bowl' of the mushrooms to fill them until level. Carefully dip the mushrooms into the breadcrumbs to cover the surface of the cheesy filling.

Place the stuffed mushrooms, breadcrumb side up, in the air fryer and cook at 180°C for 7 minutes or until bubbling and golden.

Sprinkle the chopped chives over the stuffed mushrooms before serving.

CARAMELISED ONION CHEESY GARLIC FLATBREADS

SERVES
2

These are so delicious when served with pasta or gnocchi, but equally yummy on their own. You can easily make flatbreads yourself by mixing equal parts self-raising flour and natural yogurt to form a soft dough – just follow my recipe on page 205.

Cooking time: 6 minutes

Preparation time: 5 minutes

Calories: 263 kcals per serving

For the flatbreads

2 flatbreads (or you can use pita breads)

60g mozzarella

2 tablespoons caramelised onion chutney

For the garlic butter

10g butter

1 teaspoon garlic paste

1 teaspoon dried parsley

Combine the butter with the garlic paste and dried parsley in a small bowl.

Open out the flatbreads and spread one side with the garlic butter.

Grate the mozzarella over the buttered flatbreads, then scatter a few blobs of the caramelised onion chutney over the bread.

Place the flatbreads in the air fryer. Cook at 190°C for 6 minutes or until the cheese has melted.

BAKED CAMEMBERT TEAR AND SHARE

SERVES 4

There's just something about gooey, melted cheese and fresh, crusty bread that really hits the spot, isn't there? This is the perfect sharing side for a family dinner or a night in with friends.

- Cooking time: 12 minutes
- Preparation time: 10 minutes
- Calories: 482 kcals per serving

For the Camembert

1 Camembert

4 garlic cloves, peeled

¼ teaspoon chilli flakes

¼ teaspoon dried rosemary

1 tablespoon runny honey

1 tablespoon oil

For the garlic butter

1 tablespoon butter

½ teaspoon garlic paste

To serve

1 small round crusty loaf (that fits in your air fryer)

Chopped parsley

Preheat the air fryer to 180°C.

First, cut a hole in the top of the loaf that matches the diameter and depth of the Camembert. Next, cut slices part of the way down the loaf to make it easier to pull apart once cooked.

Unwrap the Camembert, removing all the packaging, and nestle the cheese into the hole you've just made in the top of the bread.

Score the surface of the Camembert and insert the garlic cloves into the slits. Sprinkle the chilli flakes and dried rosemary over the cheese, then drizzle over the honey.

Brush the loaf all over with a little oil, place in the air fryer and cook at 180°C for 12 minutes or until the cheese has melted and the bread is lightly toasted.

Meanwhile, warm the butter and garlic in a small pan over a low heat until melted. Once ready, brush the bread all over with the garlic butter and scatter over the chopped parsley.

Place the loaf in the centre of the table for everyone to tear off a chunky of bread and dip it in the molten cheese.

BRIE AND CRANBERRY BITES

The perfect combination of savoury and sweet. These cheesy bites are such a simple but delicious dish to enjoy at any time of year, but they do make a perfect festive appetiser.

Cooking time: 15 minutes

Preparation time: 15 minutes

Calories: 125 kcals per serving

For the bites

1 sheet of ready-rolled puff pastry
(about 320g in weight)

200g Brie cheese

100g cranberry sauce

20 pecans, roughly chopped

1 egg white, lightly whisked

6 rosemary sprigs, cut into 2.5-cm pieces

24 sprays of light spray oil

Preheat the air fryer to 180°C.

Unroll the puff pastry sheet, leaving it on the parchment paper it comes on. Cut the pastry into 20 equal-sized squares.

Slice the Brie into 20 equal-sized pieces and place one piece in the centre of each pastry square.

Top the Brie on each pastry square with 1 teaspoon of cranberry sauce.

Gather up the edges of the pastry to create a little parcel, add pinch together to seal.

Brush each pastry with a little of the egg white.

Nestle a pecan on top of each pastry, along with a tiny rosemary sprig.

Place the pastry parcels in the air fryer leaving a gap between each one. Cook at 180°C for 15 minutes, or until golden. You may need to cook them in batches depending on the size of your air fryer.

Allow the bites to cool before serving.

NACHOS WITH GUACAMOLE

The perfect movie-night sharing snack, nachos loaded with spicy salsa, cool sour cream and zesty guacamole are undeniably moreish. This is such a good dish to cook in the air fryer as everything stays beautifully crisp.

Cooking time: 5 minutes

Preparation time: 10 minutes

Calories: 397 kcals per serving

For the nachos

1 x 200-g share bag of your favourite tortilla chips

100g Cheddar cheese, grated

4 tablespoons salsa

2 tablespoons jarred jalapeños (optional)

2 tablespoons sour cream, to serve

For the guacamole

1 avocado, pitted and peeled

¼ red onion, diced

50g cherry tomatoes, diced

Zest and juice of ½ lime

Small handful of chopped coriander or parsley

Salt and freshly ground black pepper

First, make the guacamole. Mash the avocado in a bowl. Add a pinch each of salt and pepper, then mix in the diced red onion and cherry tomatoes. Add a squeeze of lime juice and stir through the chopped coriander or parsley.

Preheat the air fryer to 200°C.

Line the air fryer with foil, scrunching up the sides to make a plate shape. Cover the foil with half of the tortilla chips, then scatter half of the grated cheese on top. Layer the remaining tortilla chips and grated cheese on top. Next, dot the salsa over the tortilla chips and scatter over the chopped jalapeños, if using.

Cook the nachos at 200°C for 5 minutes or until the cheese has melted.

Serve the nachos while hot with the guacamole and sour cream on the side.

COOK'S TIP

The only thing that can make this sublime snack even tastier is the addition of some leftover chilli con carne on top.

MOZZARELLA STICKS WITH MARINARA SAUCE

Oozing, cheesy goodness coated in the crispiest, golden breadcrumb coating. These molten mozzarella sticks are perfect on their own, but even better when dipped in a rich, tomatoey, marinara sauce.

⏱ Cooking time: 12 minutes

🥣 Preparation time: 10 minutes

♡ Calories: 505 kcals per serving

For the mozzarella sticks

1 block of firm mozzarella for pizza

2 tablespoons plain flour

1 teaspoon dried Italian herbs

1 egg, beaten

50g golden breadcrumbs

Salt and freshly ground black pepper

To serve

200g tomato pasta sauce from a jar (or use my Marinara Sauce recipe on page 207)

Preheat the air fryer to 160°C.

Cut the block of mozzarella into chunky sticks.

Place the flour in a bowl with ½ teaspoon of the dried herbs and season with a pinch each of salt and pepper.

Whisk the egg in a second bowl.

In a third bowl, combine the breadcrumbs with the remaining dried herbs and again season with a pinch each of salt and pepper.

First, coat the mozzarella sticks in the flour. Next, dip the sticks in the beaten egg, allowing any excess to drip away. Finally, cover the sticks in the breadcrumbs, pressing gently to make sure they are fully coated.

Place the coated mozzarella sticks in the air fryer. Spray with non-stick spray oil and cook at 160°C for 12 minutes or until golden, turning halfway through the cooking time.

Once cooked, allow the mozzarella sticks to cool for a few minutes before serving with the tomato sauce or marinara sauce as a dip.

SPRING ROLLS

SERVES
2

This Asian-inspired snack or side dish is packed with crunchy vegetables, all wrapped in thin rice paper sheets. They're simple, speedy and full of flavour – and they make a great vegetarian option.

Cooking time: 14 minutes

Preparation time: 15 minutes

Calories: 238 kcals per serving

For the spring rolls

1 carrot, very finely sliced

4 spring onions, very finely sliced

100g red cabbage, very finely sliced

30g mushrooms, finely chopped

1 teaspoon garlic paste

1 teaspoon ginger paste

1½ tablespoons dark soy sauce

6 sheets of rice paper or spring roll wrappers

Freshly ground black pepper

Non-stick spray oil

Add all of the veggies to a bowl with the garlic paste, ginger paste, ½ tablespoon of the soy sauce and a pinch of black pepper. Mix well and leave to marinate for 30 minutes.

Soak the sheets of rice paper in cold water for a few seconds.

One by one, add some of the veggie mixture to the centre of each rice paper sheet, fold in the sides and then roll up to make a spring roll. Repeat until all the rice paper sheets and veggies are used up.

Place the spring rolls in the air fryer. Spray with non-stick spray oil and cook at 180°C for 14 minutes or until crispy, turning the spring rolls halfway through the cooking time.

SAUSAGE AND CARAMELISED ONION ROLLS

MAKES
8

These sausage rolls are SO easy to make, but your friends will be really impressed when you tell them that they're homemade. The caramelised onion gives the sausage rolls a delicious sweetness, too. Yummy!

Cooking time: 14 minutes

Preparation time: 15 minutes

Calories: 306 kcals per serving

For the sausage rolls

6 thick pork sausages

2 tablespoons caramelised onion chutney

1 sheet of ready-rolled puff pastry (about 320g in weight)

1 egg, beaten

Remove the sausages from their skins and place in a bowl. Mash the sausages, then add the caramelised onion chutney and mix well together. The sausages should already be well seasoned so there's no need to add more salt and pepper.

Unroll the puff pastry sheet and slice it in half lengthways.

Divide the sausagemeat into 2 equal-sized portions. Shape each portion of sausagemeat into a long rope and place one on the side of each of the puff pastry pieces. Pull the opposite side of the pastry over the sausagemeat to enclose it. Using a fork, crimp the edges of the pastry where they meet to seal. Cut into 8 sausage rolls. Brush the sausage rolls with the beaten egg.

Preheat the air fryer to 180°C.

Place the sausage rolls in the air fryer leaving a gap between each one. Cook at 180°C for 14 minutes, or until golden and puffed up. You may need to cook them in batches depending on the size of your air fryer.

Either serve straight away while still warm or leave to cool and enjoy cold.

SCOTCH EGGS

MAKES 4

Homemade Scotch eggs are the ultimate party snack or picnic food. I love using eggs with golden yolks for that vibrant colour.

- Cooking time: 15 minutes
- Preparation time: 15 minutes
- Calories: 368 kcals per serving

For the scotch eggs

4 eggs with golden yolks

350g pork sausagemeat (or 5 thick pork sausages with skins removed)

½ teaspoon garlic paste

½ teaspoon garlic powder

2 tablespoons plain flour

1 egg

80g panko breadcrumbs

Salt and freshly ground black pepper

Non-stick spray oil

To serve

Your favourite mustard (optional)

COOK'S TIP

If you fancy a change, rather than using plain sausagemeat, you can use the meat from any flavoured sausage for a different taste.

Start by soft boiling the eggs. Lower the eggs into a pan of boiling water and cook for 6 minutes exactly. Lift the eggs out of the pan and immediately place them in iced water for 5 minutes. You can soft boil the eggs in your air fryer: I cook mine at 180°C for 8 minutes.

Once cool, peel the shells from the boiled eggs.

Preheat the air fryer to 180°C.

Place the sausagemeat in a bowl, add the garlic paste and garlic powder, then season with plenty of salt and pepper. Mix well to combine.

Divide the sausagemeat into 4 equal-sized portions. Roll each portion into a ball and then flatten it out into a round.

Place a boiled egg in the centre of each flattened sausagemeat round and pull up the meat around the egg to completely enclose it with no gaps.

Place the flour in a bowl and season with a pinch each of salt and pepper. Whisk the egg in a second bowl. In a third bowl, add the panko breadcrumbs and again season with a pinch each of salt and pepper.

First, coat the eggs in flour. Next, dip the eggs in the beaten egg, allowing any excess to drip away. Finally, cover the eggs in the panko breadcrumbs, pressing gently to make sure they are fully coated.

Place the Scotch eggs in the air fryer, spray with non-stick spray oil and cook at 180°C for 15 minutes or until golden, turning halfway through the cooking time.

Slice each Scotch egg in half to reveal the soft yolk and serve with mustard, if you like.

BUFFALO WINGS WITH RANCH DIP

MAKES 16

Coated in hot sauce and dipped in ranch dressing, these juicy chicken wings are absolutely full of flavour. Instead of being deep-fried as usual, my buffalo wings are cooked in the air fryer, which means they're juicy but not greasy. Enjoy them as a starter or a tasty snack.

⏲ Cooking time: 23 minutes

⏱ Preparation time: 10 minutes

♡ Calories: 187 kcals per serving

For the wings

1kg chicken wings

1 tablespoon baking powder

2 teaspoons smoked paprika

1 teaspoon garlic powder

1 teaspoon dried oregano

For the butter sauce

60g butter

125ml hot buffalo sauce

For the ranch dressing

4 tablespoons 'light' mayonnaise

25ml semi-skimmed milk

2 tablespoons sour cream

½ teaspoon garlic paste

½ teaspoon onion powder

½ teaspoon dried parsley

¼ teaspoon dried dill

¼ teaspoon dried or fresh chives

Salt and freshly ground black pepper

Pat dry the chicken wings, then place them in a bowl with the baking powder, paprika, garlic powder and oregano. Season the wings with plenty of salt and pepper, rubbing well to make sure the meat is fully coated.

Preheat the air fryer to 190°C.

Line the air fryer or spray with a little non-stick spray oil. Place the wings in the air fryer in a single layer, making sure they are not touching each other. Cook at 190°C for 20 minutes, flipping the wings halfway through the cooking time.

Meanwhile, make the butter sauce. Melt the butter in a small pan over a low heat with half of the hot buffalo sauce. (Reserve the rest of the buffalo sauce for serving.)

Remove the wings from the air fryer and place in a clean bowl. Pour over the butter sauce, making sure all the wings are evenly coated, and then return them to the air fryer at 190°C for 3 minutes.

Meanwhile, make the ranch dressing. Mix together all the ingredients in a bowl with a pinch each of salt and pepper.

Put the wings back in the bowl and top with the remaining hot buffalo sauce. Serve the buffalo wings with the ranch dressing for dipping.

CHAPTER
6

SWEET THINGS

BAKED OATY GOLDEN APPLES

SERVES
2

These baked apples have a buttery, oaty topping that turns deliciously crunchy in the air fryer. I like to serve them with ice cream for an easy-peasy sweet treat.

Cooking time: 15 minutes

Preparation time: 10 minutes

Calories: 257 kcals per serving

For the apples

2 Pink Lady apples

1½ tablespoons melted butter

½ teaspoon ground cinnamon

50g rolled oats

1 tablespoon golden syrup

To serve

Vanilla ice cream (optional)

Preheat the air fryer to 180°C.

Slice the apples in half and remove the cores.

Brush the cut sides of the apples with ½ tablespoon of the melted butter.

Place the apples cut side up in the air fryer and dust with the cinnamon. Cook at 180°C for 10 minutes or until the apples have softened.

Meanwhile, mix the rolled oats with 1 tablespoon of the melted butter and the golden syrup.

After 10 minutes, cover the cut sides of the apples with the oat mixture. Cook at 180°C for a further 5 minutes.

Place two apple halves in each serving bowl and add a scoop or two of vanilla ice cream to serve, if you like. Serve straight away.

RASPBERRY AND WHITE CHOCOLATE PUFF PIES

MAKES 4

Ready-rolled puff pastry is a useful ingredient for making both savoury pies and sweet desserts, I always keep a packet handy in the fridge. Puff pastry makes excellent individual pie cases that can be filled with your favourite sweet filling. Here, I've used the trusted combination of white chocolate and raspberries.

Cooking time: 20 minutes

Preparation time: 10 minutes

Calories: 474 kcals per serving

For the pies

½ sheet of ready-rolled puff pastry (about 160g in weight)

1 tablespoon butter, melted

1 egg, beaten

250g raspberries

100g white chocolate chips

150ml double cream

2 tablespoons icing sugar

Preheat the air fryer to 170°C.

Divide the pastry sheet into 4 equal-sized squares.

Brush the insides of 4 pudding tins with the melted butter to create a non-stick coating.

Push one pastry square down into each greased pudding tin to line it and create a pie case. There should be a little pastry overhanging the rims of the pudding tins.

Prick the pastry all over with the prongs of a fork, to stop it puffing up too much, and brush it all over with the beaten egg.

Place the pudding tins in the air fryer and cook at 170°C for 10 minutes or until the pastry is puffed up and golden.

Remove the pudding tins from the air fryer and ease the cooked pastry cases out of the tins. Allow to cool.

Meanwhile, make the raspberry sauce. Put 100g of the raspberries in an air-fryer safe dish and cook at 180°C for 10 minutes or until they are breaking down. Mash the raspberries and allow them to cool.

Next, make the white chocolate mousse. Melt the white chocolate in the microwave, then gently pour in 30ml of the cream and mix well. Leave it to cool to room temperature.

Whip the rest of cream with the icing sugar using a handheld electric mixer. Once whipped, gently fold in the white chocolate and cream mixture.

Spoon the white chocolate mousse into the pastry pie cases, then top with some fresh raspberries and drizzle over the raspberry sauce.

PEACH MELBA SUNDAE WITH RASPBERRY SAUCE

SERVES
2

This dessert is summer in a sundae glass. Peaches, raspberries and vanilla ice cream are the key ingredients of a Peach Melba. Here, the peaches are baked until soft and sweet, which complements the sharpness of the raspberries and milkiness of the ice cream beautifully.

Cooking time: 10 minutes

Preparation time: 10 minutes

Calories: 409 kcals per serving

For the peaches

2 peaches

1 teaspoon soft brown sugar

For the raspberry sauce

150g raspberries

1 tablespoon fresh lemon juice

3 teaspoons icing sugar

To serve

4 scoops of vanilla ice cream

Preheat the air fryer to 180°C.

Slice the peaches in half and remove the stones.

Place the peaches cut side up in a heatproof dish in the air fryer and sprinkle the brown sugar all over the cut sides of each half. Cook at 180°C for 10 minutes or until the peaches have softened. Once cool enough to handle, peel the skin from the peaches.

Meanwhile, make the raspberry sauce. Place half of the raspberries, the lemon juice and 2 teaspoons of the icing sugar in a blender, then blitz to a smooth sauce.

To assemble the peach melba, place a scoop of ice cream in the bottom of two sundae glasses or bowls. Add a peach half, followed by the fresh raspberries and then another peach half. Add another scoop of ice cream and drizzle over plenty of raspberry sauce. Serve straight away.

COOK'S TIP

For a crunchy contrast to the soft fruit and ice cream, feel free to add a handful of chopped nuts to each sundae.

BROWNIES

MAKES 8

Who doesn't love a gooey chocolatey brownie? I sure do! Once cooled, you can top the brownies with cut-up pieces of your favourite chocolate bar for extra indulgence! I like to add a sliced Mars Bar and a drizzle of caramel sauce.

Cooking time: 15 minutes

Preparation time: 15 minutes

Calories: 274 kcals per brownie

For the brownies

100g dark chocolate

100g margarine

150g golden caster sugar

60g plain flour

35g cocoa powder

2 large eggs, beaten

Your favourite chocolate bar, to decorate

Preheat the air fryer to 180°C.

Place the chocolate and margarine in a heatproof bowl and carefully microwave in a few 1 minute bursts until they have melted together. Add the sugar, flour, cocoa powder and lastly the eggs, then mix it all together until smooth.

Line a small cake tin that fits in your air fryer with parchment paper. Pour in the brownie mixture and smooth the surface to level.

Place the cake tin in the air fryer and cook at 180°C for 15 minutes.

Once cooked, place in the fridge for at least 2 hours to set.

When the brownies are set, slice up your favourite chocolate bar and scatter the pieces over the top. Lift the brownies out of the tin and slice into 8 squares.

S'MORES

MAKES
2

My daughters adore these s'mores and often request them for dessert after dinner. All kids (and big kids) enjoy this quick and easy sweet treat. You can use any favourite biscuit or type of chocolate you like.

🔔 Cooking time: 6 minutes

⏲ Preparation time: 1 minute

♡ Calories: 199 kcals per s'more

For the s'mores

4 digestive biscuits

2 medium marshmallows

2 squares milk chocolate

Place two digestive biscuits in the air fryer. Sit a marshmallow in the centre of each biscuit.

Cook in the air fryer at 180°C for 5 minutes. Depending on the air fryer, it's possible that the marshmallow may fly off. If that happens, use a toothpick to keep the marshmallow in place or switch to the baking setting rather than the air fryer mode.

Once the marshmallow has lightly browned, place a square of chocolate on the top of each melted marshmallow. Cook at 180°C for 1 minute or until the chocolate has melted.

Carefully lift the digestive biscuits out of the air fryer and place the other biscuits on top of the melted marshmallows and chocolate to make a sandwich.

COOK'S TIP

When making s'mores with chocolate-coated biscuits, remember to place the chocolate side facing upwards in the air fryer to avoid a big mess.

APPLE AND BLACKBERRY CRUMBLE

SERVES
4

Pure comfort food in a bowl. A crumble is a classic dessert that can be made with virtually any combination of fruit, including rhubarb, gooseberries, plums and pears, but I love it with the traditional combination of apples and blackberries.

Cooking time: 25 minutes

Preparation time: 15 minutes

Calories: 301 kcals per serving

For the crumble

400g Bramley apples, peeled and cut into small cubes

70g soft brown sugar

200g blackberries

50g unsalted butter, cold, cut into small cubes

100g plain flour

½ teaspoon ground cinnamon

To serve

Custard, cream or ice cream (optional)

Take the crisper tray out of the air fryer and preheat to 180°C.

Put the apples into a heatproof dish and sprinkle over 30g of the brown sugar. Cook at 180°C for 10 minutes or until the apples start to soften.

After 10 minutes, add the blackberries to the dish, mix well and cook everything for a further 5 minutes.

To make the crumble topping, combine the butter and flour in a bowl. Using your fingertips, bring the crumble topping together until it resembles large crumbs.

Add the remaining 40g of the brown sugar and the ground cinnamon to the crumble topping, then stir well.

Scatter the crumble topping over the fruit in the dish. Cook at 180°C for 10 minutes or until the crumble topping starts to turn golden all over.

Spoon the crumble into individual bowls and serve with your choice of custard, cream or ice cream, if you like.

CARAMELISED BAKED BANANAS

SERVES 2

Baking bananas brings out the natural sweetness in the fruit and turns them beautifully golden and soft. Cooked in the air fryer, bananas caramelise quickly so you can dish up a tasty dessert in no time at all.

Cooking time: 10 minutes

Preparation time: 3 minutes

Calories: 231 kcals per serving

For the bananas

2 bananas

1 tablespoon soft brown sugar

Pinch of ground cinnamon

2 scoops of vanilla ice cream

2 speculoos biscuits

2 tablespoons caramel or toffee sauce

Preheat the air fryer to 180°C.

Slice the bananas in half lengthways still in their skins.

Combine the brown sugar and cinnamon in a small bowl.

Line the air fryer. Place the bananas cut side up in the air fryer and sprinkle the cinnamon sugar all over the cut sides of each half. Cook at 180°C for 10 minutes or until the bananas are caramelised.

Place two banana halves on each serving plate with a scoop of vanilla ice cream. Crumble the biscuits over the top of each plate and drizzle over the caramel sauce. Serve straight away.

S'MORES PIE BOMBS

SERVES
4

As I've already said, my kids adore s'mores. They also love anything in pastry and so when I combined the two, it almost blew their minds! They love to help make these whenever we have everything in the cupboard for this special dessert.

Cooking time: 15 minutes

Preparation time: 10 minutes

Calories: 272 kcals per serving

For the pie bombs

½ sheet of ready-rolled puff pastry (about 160g in weight)

1 tablespoon butter, melted

1 egg, beaten

8 squares of milk chocolate

4 medium marshmallows

Icing sugar, to dust

Divide the puff pastry sheet into 4 equal-sized squares.

Brush the insides of 4 pudding tins with the melted butter to create a non-stick coating.

Push one pastry square down into each greased pudding tin to line it and create a pie case. There should be a little pastry overhanging the rims of the pudding tins.

Prick the pastry all over with the prongs of a fork, to stop it puffing up too much, and brush it all over with the beaten egg.

Place the pudding tins in the air fryer and cook at 170°C for 10 minutes or until the pastry is puffed up and golden.

Next, add 2 squares of chocolate and 1 marshmallow to each pie case. Cook for a further 5 minutes at 170°C to toast the marshmallows.

Leave the pies to cool for a few minutes, then remove them from their tins. Dust the pies with a little icing sugar before serving straight away.

BRIOCHE AND BUTTER PUDDING WITH CUSTARD

Bread and butter pudding always reminds me of my daughter's grandpa, David. He's a great cook and host, and this pudding is one of his signature dishes. Just wait until he sees how good it is when made with slices of brioche and cooked in an air fryer...

🕐 Cooking time: 15 minutes

☕ Preparation time: 10 minutes

♡ Calories: 270 kcals per serving

For the pudding

4 thick slices of brioche

100ml single cream

1 egg

1 teaspoon vanilla extract

2 tablespoons granulated white sugar

1 teaspoon butter

50g milk chocolate chips or raisins

To serve

Custard (optional)

Preheat the air fryer to 160°C.

Cut the brioche slices into even-sized cubes.

Mix together the cream, egg, vanilla extract, sugar and butter in an air-fryer safe dish.

Add the brioche cubes to the dish with the cream mixture, making sure every piece of brioche is well coated.

Scatter the chocolate chips or raisins over the brioche pieces in the dish.

Place the dish in the air fryer and cook at 160°C for 15 minutes or until golden.

Serve the pudding with custard, if you like.

STRAWBERRY AND CHOCOLATE FILO PARCELS

MAKES 8

These pretty pastry parcels are fun to make and really delicious to eat. Cooking them in the air fryer ensures that the pastry goes wonderfully crispy. I love the combination of strawberries with chocolate – a fabulous sweet treat.

Cooking time: 6 minutes

Preparation time: 10 minutes

Calories: 86 kcals per serving

For the parcels

3 sheets of filo pastry

2 tablespoons melted butter

8 squares of milk chocolate

8 strawberries, quartered, plus extra to serve

Icing sugar, to dust

Preheat the air fryer to 170°C.

Lay a filo pastry sheet out flat on a clean surface and brush it all over with melted butter.

Lay another pastry sheet over the top of the first and smooth it out.

Repeat again with the third pastry sheet.

Cut the layered pastry sheets into 8 equal-sized squares.

Place one square of chocolate in the middle of each square and some strawberry quarters. Brush a little melted butter around the edges of the pastry. Fold over to make a triangle shaped parcel, pinching the edges to seal.

Line the air fryer. Brush the parcels with a little more butter, then carefully place in the air fryer. Cook at 170°C for 6 minutes or until golden brown. Once cooked, allow the parcels to cool for 3 minutes.

Dust the parcels with icing sugar before serving with a few extra fresh strawberries on the side.

BANOFFEE PUFF PASTRY TART

The combination of bananas and toffee never fails to please. Whereas the classic banoffee pie has a biscuit base, here I use puff pastry with flaky layers beneath soft cream, and then crumble over biscuits for extra crunch. A show-stopping twist on banoffee pie, this is so easy to put together.

Cooking time: 12 minutes

Preparation time: 10 minutes

Calories: 384 kcals per serving (calorie count is based on using 160g puff pastry, but this depends on the size of your air fryer)

For the tart

½ sheet of ready-rolled puff pastry (about 160g in weight, or just enough to cover the base of your air-fryer tray)

1 egg, beaten

120ml double cream

1 tablespoon icing sugar

2 speculoos biscuits, crushed

3 bananas, sliced (or enough to cover the tart)

2 tablespoons caramel or toffee sauce

1 flaked chocolate bar

Preheat the air fryer to 170°C.

Unroll the puff pastry sheet, leaving it on the parchment paper it comes on. Cut the pastry to fit the tray of your air fryer.

Using a knife, score a border all around the edges of the pastry. Brush the pastry with the beaten egg.

Lift the pastry on its parchment paper and place in the air fryer. Cook at 170°C for 12 minutes or until the pastry is puffed up and golden. Once cooked, allow the pastry to cool completely.

Meanwhile, using a handheld electric whisk, whip the cream and icing sugar to soft peaks. Keeping it inside the border, spread the whipped cream over the pastry base.

Scatter the crushed biscuits all over the cream, then layer on the sliced bananas in neat rows. Drizzle over the caramel sauce, then crumble the flaked chocolate bar over the top. (Alternatively, grate some chocolate over the top or melt the chocolate in the microwave and drizzle it over the tart.)

Slice the tart and serve straight away.

AIR-FRYER COOKIES

MAKES 20

Whenever you need a sugar fix, these cookies can be made in minutes from ingredients that you probably already have in your storecupboard. You can use whatever type of chocolate chips you like, or make them rainbow with Smarties.

Cooking time: 8 minutes

Preparation time: 15 minutes

Calories: 215 kcals per cookie

For the cookies

220g unsalted butter, softened

100g soft brown sugar

50g granulated white sugar

1 egg, at room temperature

1 teaspoon vanilla extract

180g plain flour, sifted

1 teaspoon baking powder

½ teaspoon salt

130g milk chocolate chips

130g dark chocolate chips

First, place the butter in a mixing bowl. Add both the brown sugar and white sugar, egg and vanilla extract to the bowl and mix well to combine with the softened butter.

Next, add the flour, baking powder, salt and both milk and dark chocolate chips. Combine everything to make a soft cookie dough.

Wrap the cookie dough in clingfilm and chill in the fridge for 30 minutes.

When ready to cook, preheat the air fryer to 160°C.

Divide the cookie dough into 20 equal-sized balls and flatten them slightly. You can use an ice-cream scoop to portion out the dough so that the cookies are all roughly the same size. If you don't want to bake all the cookies at the same time, portion out the number of cookies that you need, then wrap any remaining cookie dough in clingfilm and store it in the freezer for baking on another day.

Line the air fryer. Working in batches, depending on the size of your air fryer, place the cookies in the air fryer. Leave some space around each cookie to allow for them expand. Cook at 160°C for 8 minutes or until golden.

Leave the cookies in the air fryer to cool with the door or drawer closed so they continue to cook all the way through to the middle.

BASICS

PLAIN RICE

SERVES 2

Fluffy rice makes the perfect side dish to so many different recipes. I often use microwaveable pouches of rice for maximum convenience, but it's so simple to cook your own from scratch.

Cooking time: 9 minutes

Preparation time: 3 minutes

Calories: 266 kcals per serving

For the rice

150g basmati rice

¼ teaspoon salt

350ml boiling water

Put the rice in a sieve and rinse under cold running water for 3 minutes to remove the starch from the grains.

Put the washed rice in a saucepan.

Pour over 350ml boiling water from a just-boiled kettle.

Cover the pan with a lid, bring the rice to the boil, then turn the heat down to medium-high. Make sure the water doesn't boil over the pan. Simmer the rice for 9 minutes, then drain.

Return the rice to the pan off the heat and put the lid on to steam the rice for a few minutes.

When ready to serve, fluff up the grains of rice with a fork and serve straight away.

If you have any leftover rice, cover it and place it in the fridge as soon as it is cool.

When reheating the leftover rice, make sure all the grains are piping hot throughout. I microwave mine for 5 minutes.

MEXICAN RICE

SERVES 2

This is a vibrant, flavourful rice dish, infused with the classic Mexican flavours of tomatoes, chilli and paprika. I like to serve this rice with my Tortilla Burrito Bowls (page 57).

Cooking time: 15–20 minutes

Preparation time: 10 minutes

Calories: 417 kcals per serving

For the rice

150g long-grain rice

½ x 400-g tin chopped tomatoes

½ vegetable stock cube

1 teaspoon garlic powder

½ teaspoon chilli flakes

½ teaspoon ground cumin

½ teaspoon smoked paprika (or regular paprika)

Pinch of cayenne pepper

Pinch of freshly ground black pepper

350ml boiling water

Handful of frozen peas and sweetcorn

Put the rice in a sieve and rinse under cold running water for 3 minutes to remove the starch from the grains.

Put the washed rice in a saucepan with the chopped tomatoes, stock cube and all the seasonings and spices.

Pour over 350ml boiling water from a just-boiled kettle.

Add a handful of frozen peas and sweetcorn to the pan, bring the rice to the boil, then stir well.

Cover the pan with a lid, then turn the heat down to medium. Simmer the rice for 10 minutes.

Give the rice one last good stir before serving.

CHUNKY CHIPS

SERVES 2

. . . .

Crispy on the outside and fluffy on the inside, you just can't beat home-cooked chunky chips, which go with almost any dish. Shown on page 128.

Cooking time: 22 minutes

Preparation time: 10 minutes

Calories: 376 kcals per serving

For the chips

2 baking potatoes

Non-stick spray oil

Salt and freshly ground black pepper

Preheat the air fryer to 180°C.

Slice the potatoes into chunky, thick-cut chips. (There's no need to peel the potatoes first, but you can give them a scrub if they are covered in dirt.)

Rinse the chips under cold running water, drain and pat dry with a clean tea towel.

Place the chips on a microwave-safe plate. Cook them in a microwave for 4 minutes or until partially cooked.

In a large bowl, toss the chips in some vegetable spray oil until well coated. Season with salt and pepper.

Place the chips in the air fryer, trying not to overcrowd the tray and leaving a small space between each one. Cook at 180°C for around 18 minutes or until crisp and golden, turning occasionally to make sure they cook evenly.

SWEET POTATO FRIES

Sweet potato fries are a food of the gods. Follow this recipe to get the crispiest, tastiest, air-fried sweet potato fries possible. Shown on page 117.

Cooking time: 15 minutes

Preparation time: 10 minutes

Calories: 264 kcals per serving

For the fries

2 large sweet potatoes

1 tablespoon olive oil

½ teaspoon garlic granules (or garlic powder)

½ teaspoon smoked paprika

2 tablespoons cornflour

Freshly ground black pepper

Peel the sweet potatoes, then slice them into even-sized fries. Soak the fries in a bowl of cold water for an hour to remove any excess starch, then drain and pat dry with paper towels or a clean tea towel.

Preheat the air fryer to 190°C. (This is an important step to ensure maximum crispiness.)

Put the fries in a bowl. Drizzle over the oil and toss them to coat, then add the garlic granules, paprika and a good grinding of black pepper. (Do not add any salt at this stage; you can season the fries once they're cooked.)

Now, dust the fries with the cornflour and make sure they are all evenly coated.

Place the fries in the air fryer, trying not to overcrowd the tray and leaving a small space between each one. Cook at 190°C for around 15 minutes or until crisp and golden, turning them halfway through the cooking time.

You may need to cook all the fries in batches. If so, return them all to the air fryer together at the end and cook at 190°C for a couple of minutes to reheat.

COOK'S TIP

The trick to achieving the crunchiest fries is to leave space between each one when cooking. Yes, this might mean cooking them in batches, but it's worth it for that crunch.

SMASHED GARLIC BABY POTATOES

There's nothing better than a garlicky, smashed potato with an extra cheesy hit of Parmesan. They're the absolute perfect side for so many dishes. Smashing the potatoes underneath a glass before popping them in the air fryer breaks them open and increases the surface area for maximum crispiness.

Cooking time: 35 minutes

Preparation time: 10 minutes

Calories: 225 kcals per serving

For the potatoes

350g baby potatoes

1 tablespoon melted butter

1 teaspoon garlic paste

1 tablespoon chopped parsley

30g Parmesan cheese, grated

Place the baby potatoes in a large saucepan of salted water. Bring the potatoes to the boil over a medium heat and cook for 10 minutes or until just tender.

Preheat the air fryer to 180°C.

Once cool enough to handle, take each par-boiled baby potato, place a heavy-based drinking glass on top and press down to 'smash' the potato.

In a small bowl, combine the melted butter with the garlic paste and chopped parsley leaves.

Line the air fryer. Place the smashed baby potatoes in the air fryer and brush them all over with the garlic-parsley butter. Scatter over the grated Parmesan.

Cook the smashed potatoes at 180°C for 25 minutes or until crispy and golden on the outside.

FLATBREADS

A quick and easy recipe for a basic but versatile flatbreads. Left plain these flatbreads are the perfect accompaniment to a main dish or try spreading with my Marinara Sauce (page 207) for a cheat's pizza, which you can customise with your favourite toppings.

Cooking time: 8 minutes

Preparation time: 10 minutes

Calories: 498 kcals per serving

For the flatbreads
100g self-raising flour

Pinch of salt

100g full-fat Greek yogurt

Non-stick spray oil

Combine the flour and salt in a mixing bowl. Stir in the yogurt to make a rough dough.

Separate the dough into 2 equal-sized balls.

On a lightly floured work surface, roll out each ball of dough to make the flatbreads. If the dough sticks to the surface or rolling pin, dust with a little extra flour.

Preheat the air fryer to 180°C.

Spray the air fryer with spray oil, spreading it with a brush if necessary.

Place the flatbreads in the air fryer. Cook at 180°C for 4 minutes. After 4 minutes, flip the flatbreads over, spray them again with oil, then cook for a further 4 minutes or until golden.

WHITE SAUCE OR CHEESE SAUCE

SERVES 6

A classic white sauce is quick to whip up, but it's so versatile. It's great to use in pasta dishes, such as lasagne and gnocchi bolognese, or you can add grated Cheddar to make a cheese sauce that is perfect for cauliflower cheese.

Cooking time: 12 minutes

Preparation time: 5–6 minutes

Calories: 127 kcals per serving of white sauce, 170 kcals per serving of cheese sauce

For the sauce

50g butter

50g flour

500ml semi-skimmed milk

100g Cheddar cheese (optional)

Whole nutmeg

Salt and freshly ground black pepper

Start by melting the butter in a saucepan over a low heat.

Gradually add the flour to the pan, continuously whisking it into the melted butter to make a smooth paste.

Next, gradually add the milk to the pan and slowly whisk it into the paste to make a thick sauce.

If making a cheese sauce, add the grated Cheddar and slowly whisk it into the sauce.

Add a pinch each of salt and pepper and grate in a little nutmeg, to taste.

COOK'S TIP

To make a quick and tasty cauliflower cheese, place separated cauliflower florets in a heatproof dish and roast in the air fryer at 180°C for 15 minutes or until starting to soften. Pour over the cheese sauce, top with a little more grated Cheddar, then cook in the air fryer again for a further 2 minutes.

MARINARA SAUCE

A great sauce for making authentic pasta dishes or use it to top my homemade flatbreads for a quick pizza. You can use plum tomatoes for this sauce instead of passata, just squish them with your hands when adding them to the pan.

Cooking time: 12 minutes

Preparation time: 10 minutes

Calories: 53 kcals per serving

For the sauce

1 onion, diced

1 teaspoon garlic paste (or 2 garlic cloves, chopped)

Non-stick spray oil

1 teaspoon dried oregano

½ teaspoon chilli flakes (optional)

1 tablespoon balsamic vinegar

1 x 500-g carton tomato passata

1 teaspoon sugar

Handful of fresh basil leaves, torn

Salt and freshly ground black pepper

Peel and dice the onion. Put the diced onion in a large saucepan, add the garlic paste and a few sprays of spray oil. Cook the onion and garlic for 5–6 minutes, or until softened but not coloured.

Once the onion has softened, stir in the dried oregano and chilli flakes, if using. Add the balsamic vinegar, then pour in the tomato passata. Stir well.

Simmer for 3 minutes, then stir in the sugar and torn basil leaves. Season with salt and pepper.

Simmer for a further 3 minutes or until the sauce has reduced and thickened.

CHILLI JAM

MAKES 3 JARS

This homemade jam (although it's actually more of a jelly) adds a sweet chilli kick to so many dishes. It's the perfect accompaniment to serve with cheese toasties, burgers, wraps, and even with cheese and crackers, so make a batch to keep this addictive chilli jam in stock. It's easy to double up the recipe if you want to make more jars, which make excellent gifts for foodie friends.

Cooking time: 20 minutes

Preparation time: 10 minutes

Calories: 50 kcals per tablespoon

For the chilli jam

5 red chillies

15g red jalapeños from a jar, drained

1 garlic clove

½ red pepper

500g jam sugar (with pectin)

250ml cider vinegar

You will also need:

3 x 190-ml jam jars

Chop the tops off the red chillies and discard. Place the chillies in a food processor, then add the drained red jalapeños and garlic clove. Blitz until all the ingredients are well combined.

Cut the red pepper in half. Remove the stem and seeds, then roughly chop the pepper. Add the chunks of pepper to the food processor and blitz again.

Put the jam sugar and cider vinegar in a very large saucepan. Warm over a medium heat for 10 minutes or until all the sugar has dissolved. Do NOT stir the mixture at any point before, during or after heating.

After 10 minutes, add the red chilli and pepper mixture to the pan, turn the heat up and boil for a further 10 minutes. Again, do NOT stir the mixture.

After 10 minutes, remove the pan from the heat and leave the chilli jam to cool – this will take at least 30 minutes.

While the chilli jam cools, sterilise the jam jars. Wash the jars in hot soapy water. Rinse the jars, then put them in the air fryer. Heat the jars at 150°C until they're completely dry.

Once cool, pour the chilli jam into the sterilised jars and seal tightly with the lids.

When kept in a cool, dark cupboard, the jars of chilli jam can be stored for up to 1 month.

COOK'S TIP

It's crucial that you do NOT stir the contents of the saucepan while making this chilli jam. Stirring disturbs the sugar crystals, which means the jam won't set properly.

TOMATO KETCHUP

MAKES 2 JARS

Whether it's a squirt on the side of a fry up or a dollop for dipping chunky chips, tomato ketchup has to be the nation's favourite sauce. It's a classic condiment that is even tastier when homemade.

Cooking time: 1 hour 15 minutes

Preparation time: 10 minutes

Calories: 45 kcals per serving

For the ketchup

2kg tomatoes

2 onions

2 garlic cloves

150ml red wine vinegar

2 bay leaves

½ teaspoon black peppercorns

½ dried red chilli, crushed

1 tablespoon soft light brown sugar

You will also need:
2 x 190-ml jam jars

Start by roughly chopping the tomatoes and peeling and slicing the onions and garlic. Put them in a large saucepan and add 50ml of the red wine vinegar and 100ml cold water. Cook over a medium heat for 40 minutes or until the tomatoes have broken down and reduced.

Meanwhile, pour the remaining 100ml red wine vinegar in another saucepan and add the bay leaves, black peppercorns and dried red chilli. Simmer over a low heat for 10 minutes, then remove the pan from the heat and set aside.

Using a handheld stick blender, blitz the tomato mixture in the pan until smooth. Next, pass it through a sieve to ensure all the skins and seeds are removed to leave a smooth tomato purée, then return it to the pan.

Pour the infused vinegar into the main pan with the strained tomato purée and add the sugar. Bring the ketchup to the boil over a medium heat, stirring frequently to dissolve the sugar.

Lower the heat and reduce to a simmer until the ketchup has reduced and thickened to your preferred consistency.

Remove the pan from the heat and leave the tomato ketchup to cool.

While the ketchup cools, sterilise the jam jars. Wash the jars in hot soapy water. Rinse the jars, then put them in the air fryer. Heat the jars at 150°C until they're completely dry.

Once cool, pour the ketchup into the sterilised jars and seal tightly with the lids.

When kept in a cool, dark cupboard, the jars of tomato ketchup can be stored for up to 1 month.

INDEX

A

B

ACKNOWLEDGEMENTS

First of all, thank you to Ru Merritt at Ebury Press for making this book possible. Your advice throughout has been invaluable. My thanks also go to Lucinda Humphrey for all her assistance on the editorial side. And not forgetting Francesca Thomson in publicity and Lara McLeod in marketing for their work in promoting this book.

I would like to thank Lisa Pendreigh for being the most supportive editor. I simply could not have done all this without you. Thank you for your patience!

I have to thank the photography team who have brought all my recipes to life on these pages. To photographer Hannah Hughes, food stylist Amy Stephenson and props stylist Lauren Miller, I couldn't love the photos any more.

To Studio Noel, thank you for the amazing design of the book and bringing everything together on the pages.

To my family. I want to say thanks to my parents for always supporting and believing in me. I've learnt so much from the two of you! To my sister, who is my best friend and absolute rock. Thanks for always being there for me. To Gran Jan, who is like a second mum to me and the best gran to my girls. Thank you for always being there to support us. And to my daughters, I hope you're as proud of me as I am of you. This is all for you two.

Finally, a massive thank you to all of you. Thanks for following and supporting my journey. None of this would have happened without you.

ABOUT THE AUTHOR

Hayley Dean

For the past eight years, Hayley has been sharing her quick and easy recipes online through her TikTok and Instagram accounts. With a young family, she knows just how difficult it can be to eat well when you have little time, so Hayley's focus has always been on creating tasty recipes that are super easy to make.

Hayley has been obsessed with cooking for as long as she can remember. Entirely self-taught, Hayley has always experimented in the kitchen, often creating quick and easy versions of many of her favourite restaurant and takeaway dishes at home.

Hayley was quick to embrace the air fryer as she immediately realised this kitchen gadget's potential to serve up wholesome family food in record time.

Hayley's delicious, home-cooked, air-fryer recipes always hit the spot and have gained her an enthusiastic and loyal audience. Her air-fryer recipes for Pizza Toasties, Peri-Peri Chicken Burgers, Chicken Tenders and Hunter's Chicken have all gone viral and to date have received over 10 million views. You can find Hayley and all the delicious food that she makes on Instagram at hayleys.world.

Many of Hayley's most-viewed popular recipes, along with lots and lots of brand new ones, have now been gathered together in this book for you to make the most of your air fryer. This is Hayley's first cookbook.

13

Ebury Press, an imprint of Ebury Publishing
20 Vauxhall Bridge Road, London SW1V 2SA

Ebury Press is part of the Penguin Random House group of companies
whose addresses can be found at global.penguinrandomhouse.com

First published by Ebury Press in 2023

www.penguin.co.uk

A CIP catalogue record for this book is available from the British Library.

ISBN 9781529915723

Project Editor: Lisa Pendreigh
Designers: Studio Noel
Photographer: Hannah Hughes
Food Stylist: Amy Stephenson
Props Stylist: Lauren Miller

Colour origination by Altaimage Ltd, London
Printed and bound in Great Britain by Bell and Bain Ltd, Glasgow

The authorised representative in the EEA is Penguin Random House
Ireland, Morrison Chambers, 32 Nassau Street, Dublin D02 YH68

Penguin Random House is committed to a
sustainable future for our business, our readers
and our planet. This book is made from Forest
Stewardship Council® certified paper.